mise-en-scène
\ ,mē-,zä^{n}-'sen, -'sän \
pl mise-en-scènes

1 a: the process of putting a play or other theatrical production on the stage : the arrangement of the scenery, properties, and actors onstage <the mise-en-scène suggested that nobody had had much rehearsal —Winthrop Sargeant> <a mise-en-scène that included eight horses galloping onstage in the last act —John Briggs> b: STAGE SETTING <a shabby, down-at-the-heels mise-enscène that scarcely could be called decor —Saturday Rev.> <spectacle plays attempted a more realistic, three-dimensional mise-en-scène —A.N. Vardac>

2 a: the physical setting of an action <gaze on this ordinary house that became the mise-en-scène of an extraordinary drama —E.M. Lustgarten> b: ENVIRONMENT, MILIEU <the books of chivalry... were part of the Spanish mise-en-scène —New Yorker>

Webster's Third New International Dictionary

Mise-en-Scène

Mise-en-Scène

The Lives and Afterlives of Urban Landscapes

Chris Reed
Mike Belleme

ORO EDITIONS

LIMIT OF WORK
LIMIT OF WORK
LIMIT OF WORK
LIMIT OF WORK
+LP 849
+HP 853
+LP 847.5
+LP 844
+HP 852
+HP 848
+LP 847.5
BIG EVENT TENT
BIG STAGE
BELL TOWER.
GARDEN
GARDEN

+HP 849.5
+LP 850
+HP 853
LIMIT OF WORK
+HP 855
855
854
853
852
851
850
+HP 848
+LP 844
P 852.5
+HP 847
+LP 847.5
LIMIT OF WORK
NORTH

All the cities are one city. What is interesting to find, in this continuity of cities, the less obvious differences of texture: the signs, the markings, the assemblages, the things hiding in plain sight in each cityscape or landscape: the way streetlights and traffic signals vary, the most common fonts, the slight variations in building codes, the fleeting ads, the way walls are painted, the noticeable shift in the range of hues that people wear, the color of human absence, the balance of industrial product versus what has been made by hand, greater or lesser degrees of finish, the visual melody of infrastructure as it interacts with terrain: wall, roof, plant, wire, gutter: what is everywhere but is everywhere slightly different.

Teju Cole

Setting the Stage: The Social Lives of Urban Landscapes

Chris Reed

Photo by Jules Allen

Kids are amazing. They come with no pretenses, few preconceptions, few socializations. They don't know things in the way that they will as they grow up, they don't understand that certain things have certain uses—they encounter the stuff of the world for what it is: shapes, colors, tastes, smells, sounds, three-dimensional figures in space—all things to touch, to taste, to smell, to kick, to sit on, maybe to lick, to play with, even to test and challenge, and to explore on their own terms.

My own children, early on, would create an adventure of simply walking down the street. As many of us have, they would make games around sidewalk cracks, and of hopping from one utility cover to the next, completely unaware that these heavy, dark discs in the paving were portals to an infrastructural underworld that powers and services the city. Curious, they responded unabashedly to the world they encountered, exploring their environment through their senses, before they were conditioned to understand functions, relations, associations, customs. They invented uses and meaning for themselves.

This unselfconscious appropriation of things has always fascinated me. In school we were often told to sit still, sit up straight, not to lean back—as if there were only one way to sit, as if we were all comfortable in standard-issue school furniture, and even though we all have different body sizes and shapes. Certain seats are more comfortable for some of us than for others. And sometimes we want to sit improperly, to slouch, lounge, or relax, or sit with someone in our lap. We find different ways to sit on a log, lie on a lawn or at the beach, recline against a tree. We adapt to the conditions around us and put them to unintended use to suit our purposes. This is what is happening in Herman Hertzberger's photo of two ladies, lunching in front of a cafe and sandwiched between two parked cars rather than in the cafe itself or as part of the cafe's sidewalk seating.

Photo by Herman Hertzberger

People like them find their own place in this world. We appropriate the stuff around us and adapt it and our own bodies to the tasks or desires at hand.

In the 1970s, William Whyte extensively studied the behavioral and social tendencies of people as well as our ability to adapt flexibly and shared his findings in his *The Social Life of Small Urban Spaces* (1980). Whyte's studies of the ways in which people gathered on the plaza and ledge in front of Mies van der Rohe's

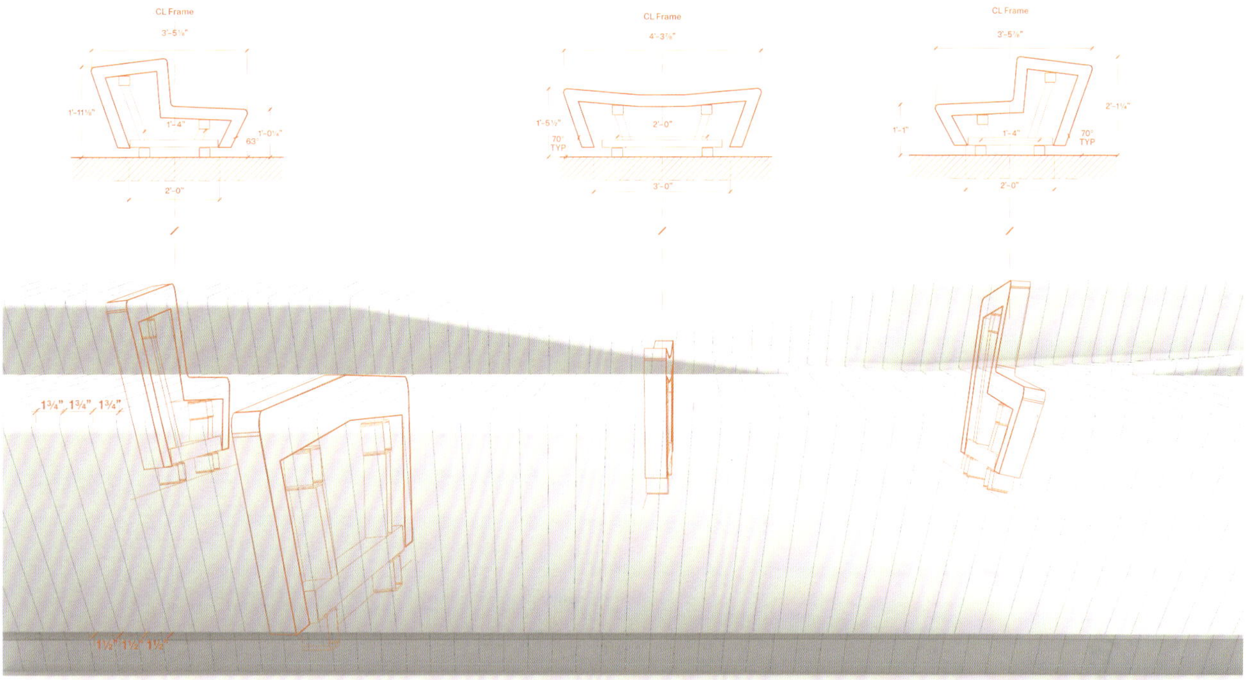

Harvard Science Center Plaza Benches, drawing by Stoss

Seagram Building in New York, for example, highlighted human, behavioral adaptations to this particular space and its environment, and demonstrated more broadly how people can and want to act in the public realm of the city. Whyte studied the evolving relationships of people's chosen sitting and gathering locations on the plaza and then mapped his findings with changing sunlight and shade over the course of the day; to work and lunch and commuting schedules; and to each other—noting how folks would use the space differently at different times and in response to different microclimatic conditions and social schedules.

This work is significant to me as a watchful observer of people and the urban scene and of the unfettered ways in which people interact with their settings and with each other. It is also significant to me as a designer to understand how what we design—whether a bench, a public space, or an entire district of the city—might pick up on the innate, behavioral characteristics and habits of people (and of larger social/environmental systems and dynamics) as a starting point for thinking about how we shape people's environments.

Photo by Mike Belleme

As informants to physical design, we can learn by observing closely, and we can anticipate by applying our research. Choice, diversity, flexibility, and adaptability—of designed elements and spaces and of the people who will come to inhabit them—are critical informants for a place to be conducive to richly changing social and collective uses. But we must also leave room for the unanticipated, the unexpected—and those things that are simply beyond our control.

These understandings of human character and human behavior, gained through observing the *mise-en-scène* closely, inform the way that I and (and we at Stoss) approach our work, approach the lives of the cities and projects and people we engage. And they inform the thinking behind our work at places like the Science Center Plaza at Harvard, depicted here and in the Boston chapter—at both the scale of the human body (through the design of custom seating) and at the scale of the site (through the design and programming of the plaza itself). They are also behind others' speculative, urban-scale propositions for the city, such as OMA's 1991 Yokohama Masterplan, and in many public spaces around the world, many of which were documented by Cannon Ivers in *Staging Urban Landscapes* (2018). Many of Mike Belleme's *Mise-en-Scène* photographs capture the rich, social dynamics and urban-environmental conditions that we play off as designers and urban strategists; they document the lives of the places where we work, the afterlives of some of the places we have designed, the social and environmental dynamics that the renovations we imagine and design have activated. More so, they capture the scenes and conditions of contemporary American cities, the things people do and the places they do them in—at least just before the COVID-19 pandemic descended upon us in early 2020. These real-life stages and the people and scenes depicted are the focal points of this project.

—

I grew up in a small city in the northeast, on the water, a city of immigrants and of workers. My Dad was a funeral director, my Mom was a nurse-turned-homemaker and volunteer. My home town of New Bedford is an oddly shaped city: fourteen miles north to south but only one or two miles at most east to west. Much of the city's eastern edge lies along the Acushnet River, a tidal river and estuary that empties into Buzzards Bay and then the Atlantic Ocean; the southern tip of the city narrows as a peninsula, with public beaches that we frequently visited during especially hot and humid summers. My experience of the city included hanging out in a public park, within a half-mile of my house, with both open and wooded areas—the latter good for exploring the only "nature" we knew—and kicking down the cobbled and gaslamped streets of the historic district, which harken back to the city's whaling days, and around a partly vacated downtown nearby. The fishing wharves on the harbor were our center of activity, though, with dozens of boats landing their catch of Atlantic white fish and scallops. It was a boom and bust city—from whaling to manufacturing to fishing—a city always suffering from the last decline even as the next wave of work and sustenance was taking its place, employing some but not all.

Our typical adventure was to walk along an access road on the city's enormous hurricane dike, built after a number of hurricanes in the first part of the twentieth century, to an island that was only accessible at low tide. Palmer's Island seemed a world away from the city, in the middle of the harbor, but still within earshot of the working wharves. It offered scrambles through low brush and along the beach to an abandoned lighthouse at the far tip of the island. Ours was an urban adventure in a watery wildlands with maritime ruins, but always with views to the city. And as much as it was an amazing escape for a teenager, it was always full of a little tension: would we make it back before the tide filled in again?

Years later I learned that the same hurricane dike that I used to walk to the island contributed to the slow poisoning of the harbor and river mouth. The contaminated river bottom was in fact a cruel collaboration between the waste of upriver manufacturing operations that sustained the city after the industrial revolution and the protective infrastructure constructed in the twentieth century at the mouth of the harbor to shield those factory mills from storm. By the time I was exploring the island in the 1980s, most of the mills were quiet, and their toxic residue had settled to the river bottom never to be flushed to sea because of the narrow opening in the hurricane dike.

Later, as a university student, I came to realize the city I grew up in was very much caught up in larger economic and environmental struggles. It was a city whose primary economies were always tied directly to its environmental setting, whether its protected, deep port or its abundance of water that could help power and supply industrial manufacturing. Its best intentions—to put people to work and then to protect those assets—resulted in one of the largest environmental disasters on the east coast of the US, culminating in New Bedford's river and harbor being designated a Superfund site by the US Environmental Protection Agency in 1982.

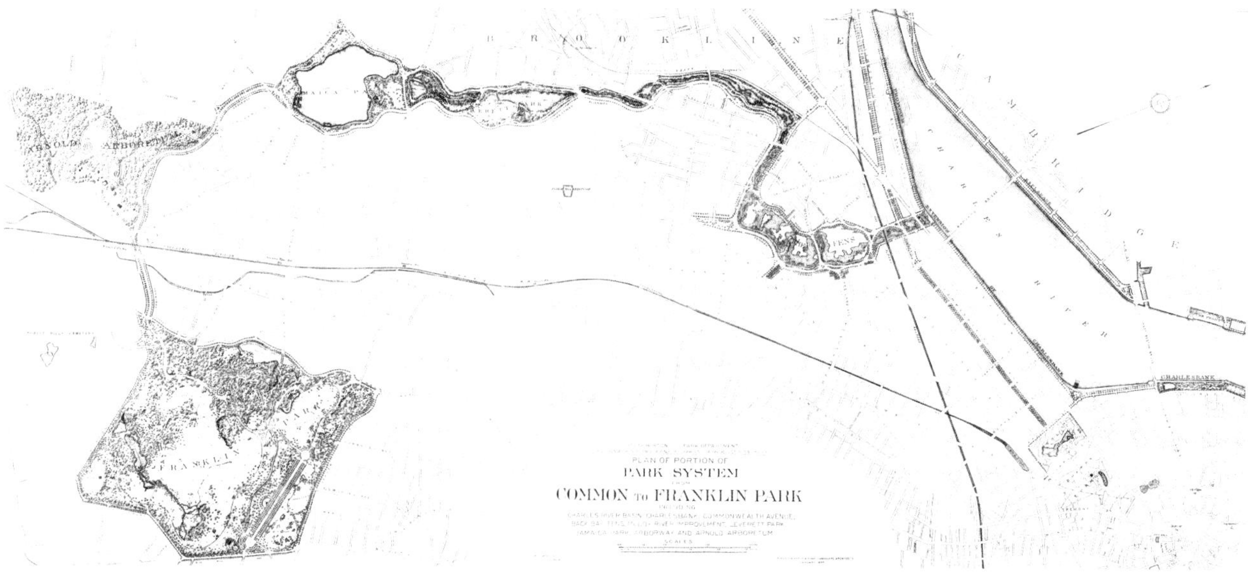

Plan of Emerald Necklace Park System in Boston by Frederick Law Olmsted

Photo by Lewis Wickes Hine

The confluence of work, recreation, ecology, infrastructure, and environmental crisis at the heart of a city, as well as the challenges of industrialization and infrastructural ambitions, make it a place caught up in some of the same struggles cities face today. This confluence also describes my entry point to design and to landscape in particular. For me, landscape was never a horticultural pursuit—though, admittedly, I did learn from my grandmother how to properly plant a perennial as I helped to tend her small garden in South Dartmouth. I also did not start into landscape because it was somehow an extension of the environmental movements of the 1970s and 1980s, though there was something of interest to me here about the ways in which landscape was tied to larger-scale ecological forces as well as environmental and public health. Rather, the landscapes that captured my imagination were very much like that complicated working harbor landscape of my childhood—urban, industrialized, transformed—yet still living, still dynamic, still offering the opportunity to connect to something deep, something wild, something guttural, something sensual.

But it wasn't until I discovered the American parks movement of the late nineteenth century that something clicked. I learned that Frederick Law Olmsted and his contemporaries imagined entire park systems for cities such as Boston, Buffalo, Minneapolis, and Seattle—park systems that were at once recreational amenities and escapes, new forms of urban habitat, flood control measures, and transportation and mobility infrastructure (with integrated light rail systems and new roads and carriage-ways). In this sense, these park systems reorganized the ways in which cities worked, reshaped urban form around parks and landscape infrastructures, and physically touched the lives of an incredible number of people. They were also born of robust social reform efforts at the time, various initiatives that were aimed at improving the health and social conditions of the poorest city residents who did not have access to clean air and water and to nature within the rapidly expanding industrial city.

All this—the impact and implication of landscape in the heart of the city and as a shaper of city-life, at a wide range of scales from the individual person to the larger ecosystem—is where I see landscape and the lives of cities converging. City life, urban infrastructure, social

Photo by Jules Allen

Photo by Frank Gohlke

networks, and ecological dynamics are, together, the starting point for our work at Stoss and for what we try to instigate, initiate, or interact with as we design and program public space projects. They also represent the larger scene within which our work—and life itself in the contemporary American city—is set.

—

My life has grown more complex over the past two decades. I have three interracial kids (including two 6'-1" boys who read as Black) growing up in a post-Ferguson, post-Trayvon Martin world, but in the relatively safe and liberal town of Brookline, Massachusetts, right in the heart of the Boston area. Within this seemingly innocuous setting, my Black wife has been challenged by police officers on our own property, and on Brookline's main commercial street we've witnessed Black motorists stopped for no apparent reason. Yet my kids live an otherwise privileged life in what we generally consider an open, multi-ethnic, and somewhat multiracial community. Like many other parents in far more threatening circumstances, I have deep concerns paired with an enormous amount of hope and optimism about the lives my kids are leading and will lead, about the opportunities and challenges all three of them have ahead. Will their skills, intellects, efforts, and personalities bring them the rewards of a happy and productive life, or will skin-deep judgments, policies, and perceptions negatively affect what they can and will do, or worse?

Racial prejudices and social inequities run deep across America and around the world, and continue to have a negative impact on the daily lives of and opportunities for young black- and brown-skinned people throughout the US and for immigrant and migrant populations nationally and globally. The last few decades have seen unprecedented advances in race relations and public discourse on the social and economic inequities built into systems of government, politics, and other institutions—and yet much of the hatred and contempt behind these historic injustices (fueled especially by a President whose power and authority seem to rest on chaos and inequity) has also surfaced publicly. In the spring of 2020 with its pandemic-infused restlessness and frustration, systemic racism has reemerged front and center in American life, triggered once again by the senseless killings of Black people by police. Optimistically, it has also inspired a wave of protest and activism—with a demand that we consider how institutional power and decision-making benefit some at the economic and health expense of others. Societal and political concerns are only one part of all the work that has yet to be done.

On other fronts, cities, people, the environment, the globe are all fraught with rapidly increasing challenges, brought to a head by political and economic forces that maybe are not always looking out for everyone's best interests. These tensions, between societal, racial, and environmental advancement and retreat, the battle for the hearts and minds of people, continue to play out in so many of today's public discussions, especially about new development, open space, and planning and design strategies in cities. This is where broader societal questions and battles—very

Drawing of current and projected storm surge events at Galveston Seawall by Stoss, atop photo by Mike Belleme

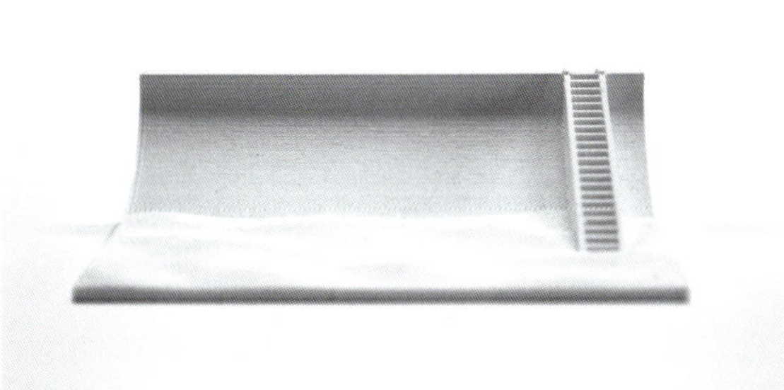

Galveston Seawall, model by Stoss

much in play in the world at large as well—infuse my professional work, my teaching, and my day-to-day life as husband, father, and city-dweller. And this book is where those lines come together: a photojournalist's depictions of the people and urban landscapes of seven cities across the US intersecting with the work we do at Stoss, and as impacted by the politics and racist planning policies, currently looking forward from the COVID pandemic, ongoing racist attacks, social unrest.... The stages on which we work, the actors we engage with, are already in motion when we arrive. Our work begins many acts in, and our appearances are sometimes relatively short. You might think of our work as understanding the scripts and dialogues as they are playing themselves out; interacting with those on stage and the forces behind the scenes in ways that both respond to and shift what is at work; re-setting the trajectory of the play in ways that sometimes reveals what is hidden; and giving new voice to those who have been off stage—all allowing for new and healthier interactions among urban dwellers, their cities, and the environments in which they live.

—

Mise-en-Scène is about the social lives of cities and the people who live in them—and the urban, social, political, cultural, and environmental contexts in which they are situated. Its photographs document, interrogate, and tease out the issues, tensions, joys, everyday activities, celebrations, and intimate moments of people—people who are getting by, looking for opportunities, looking for social interactions of various sorts and for moments to explore and to be liberated, or looking just to be themselves.

It's a book about the diverse and complex issues that shape and impact cities today: current and impending effects of climate change, rapid economic redevelopment, potential displacement, homelessness, increasing cultural and ethnic diversity, social and racial inequities, social and cultural life. This book is about life itself: our lives lived and experienced as urban dwellers, as sentient, animate human beings, as social beings, as belonging to the flora and fauna of an increasingly changing and challenging environment. And it's a book about what we, as designers, landscape architects, and urban strategists at Stoss encounter in our everyday worklives. The lives and situations depicted in the photographs here *set the stage* for the work we do in cities, just as our designs and projects set up new or altered conditions that themselves prompt new responses, new actions, new dynamics, new scenes that continue to play out long after we leave.

Belleme's photographs not only intimate where we begin as designers and urban strategists; they also document the afterlives of the places we have designed or that our designs have activated. *Mise-en-Scène*'s accompanying drawings depict this in relationship to the physical features and infrastructures we discover on a site: the Galveston sea wall, for instance, with the many, local, current, and projected levels of tides, rising seas, and storm surges. They depict the very physical elements that we as designers have direct control over, such as a bench, wetland terraces, a civic plaza, and the like, and that we articulate to both respond to those underlying conditions and set off an entirely new set of social and environmental dynamics that we hope will contribute to a richer, healthier, more robust urban landscape.

More importantly, this is a book about contemporary urban life in the American city. Belleme's photographs offer scenes from a pre-pandemic urban America from the standpoint of a photojournalist, in keeping with a lineage of street photographers that date back over a century. The five interspersed essays by contributors whose backgrounds range from curator to ecologist, from designer to social advocate and artist to critic, were written during the pandemic and the many calls for social and racial justice for Blacks and for all non-white people. The Stoss drawings capture the wide range of scales and environments that we work in, and illustrate especially the ways we document our proposals for projects intended to work with the dynamic milieus in which we work. They capture the multiple tools and techniques we use to analyze, communicate, and project—and focus on those parts of a project or collaboration that we control, that we inscribe—with the hope of triggering anew the social and environmental forces that are in play. Quotations from a broad canvas of literary, design, and environmental writings bring forward some of the intellectual and cultural provocations of *Mise-en-Scène*; short outtakes from city-dwellers involved in the outreach and engagement processes around Stoss's work provide a real-world perspective from a multitude of competing voices that are at work informing the futures of these places.

In this way, *Mise-en-Scène* is a bit of a scrapbook, a collection of artifacts and documents that are not necessarily intended to create logical narratives, more intended as a curated collection of stuff that might reverberate, one thing off another, to offer multiple readings, multiple musings, multiple futures on city-life. While design is present here and there in the drawings and some of the texts and photographs, the book captures the broad contexts in which designers work and the issues we face in contemporary cities and politics—and therefore addresses a broader audience of city-lovers, photography buffs, activists, sociologists, cultural aficionados, art lovers, and critics. It is intended to engage others in conversation about cities and landscapes to ultimately continue to inform the ways in which we, as designers, can think and work—and deliberately not limit those conversations to our own circles in design.

Mise-en-Scène, then, turns to the physical and social conditions of seven distinct cities across the United States—Los Angeles, Galveston, St. Louis, Green Bay, Ann Arbor, Detroit, and Boston. It explores the social lives that they give rise to, sometimes in spite of the environmental, social, cultural, political, and economic circumstances around. A collaboration between Mike Belleme, a photojournalist, and me, a landscape architect and urbanist, this book brings to light the challenges, tensions, hopes, special moments, and everyday activities of people who live and work in contemporary cities. It pictures some of the social, cultural, environmental, and economic challenges and changes that cities around

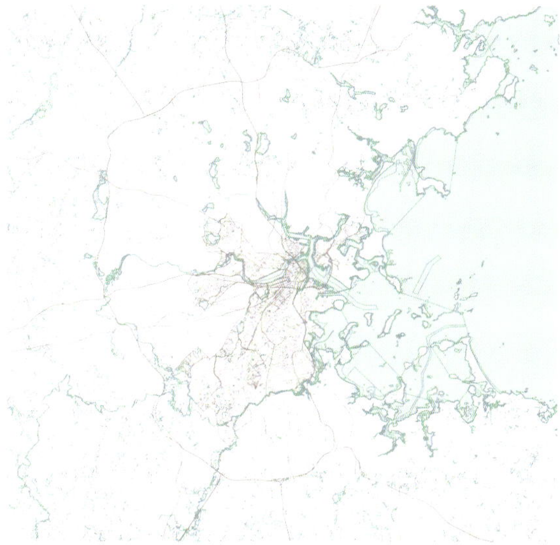

Map of Boston by Stoss

Photo by Ansel Adams

Photo by Edward Burtynsky

the world are facing today. It suggests both starting points for and some aftereffects of design work in the public realm, work that must confront both the realities of contemporary urbanism (including climate change, social and racial tensions, rapid development, and multiculturalism) and create new opportunities for everyday common grounds and places for all of us to interact directly with one another.

These seven contemporary American cities range in terms of size, geography, politics, ambitions, and character. They represent a national cross-section but are somewhat serendipitous in that they are places where the Stoss Landscape Urbanism practice has worked over the past decade on strategic planning and design projects. In *Mise-en-Scène*, a west to east arrangement of cities, from Los Angeles to Boston, is meant to facilitate comparison and contrast. A curated set of maps, drawings, and diagrams by Stoss relate the various modes and methodologies invoked in crafting public spaces to respond to the conditions in Belleme's photographs and to set up conditions for new forms of human interaction.

This book offers a more expansive idea of the potential influences on and implications or effects of design disciplines regularly practicing in and thinking about cities. While these cities are quite different from one another in terms of geography, size, population, people, climate, economics, ethnic composition, cultural heritage, lifestyles, etc., this project speaks to a remarkable interconnectedness across these geographies, scales, and situations: that the tensions invoked by a redeveloping and inundated waterfront in East Boston shares a story or a lineage with an emerging set of conversations on race and identity in St. Louis, with an impromptu workers' rally on a beach in Los Angeles, or with White families living off the land in a predominantly Black Detroit; or that increasingly frequent street flooding faced by residents of Galveston Island is tied to the same forces that guide the design of a stormwater garden in Ann Arbor and a dry courtyard in Venice Beach; or that the detail of a bench in Green Bay shares an origin story with a mattress stuffed under an old bleacher in a Boston park, or with teenagers sprawled on a dock in Michigan. These kinds of connections are offered implicitly through the imagery of the different cities, and explicitly through drawings and cross-referencing around topics including ecology, water, social space, housing, and infrastructure. Introductory maps of each city, provided at a consistent scale for easy

Photo by Alex S. MacLean

comparison, describe the environmental and infrastructural systems in each place; they are in many ways foundational to how each city functions.

This work is intended to record a moment in time, to prompt reflection on possibilities and paths forward for those in and out of the planning and design disciplines, and to spark conversation and speculation among those who love and work and live in cities, and the hopes and challenges they face.

—

Landscape photography and the photography of urban street scenes have shaped public perceptions for many decades and have often played important roles in advocating for issues of the day. Ansel Adams' photographs of Yosemite and the future national parks, for instance, helped make Americans aware of these awe-inspiring landscapes and were used to apply political pressure to preserve them in perpetuity. Edward Burtynsky's haunting photographs of contaminated and working landscapes toward the end of the twentieth century inspired new, environmental initiatives to clean up degraded landscapes of this sort and take measures to avoid causing such harm to the environment in the future. Much earlier, urban street photographers such as Jacob Riis were credited with helping to urge on significant social reform efforts in the latter half of the nineteenth century, a movement that ultimately led to the public park movement in the United States. This relationship between photography and landscape architecture was poignantly featured in "Big Plans: Picturing Social Reform," an exhibit co-curated by Charles Waldheim and Sara Zewde at the Isabella Stewart Gardner Museum in Boston in 2019, in which they juxtaposed photographs by social reformers and large park and landscape plans created by Frederick Law Olmsted and others in New York, Chicago, and Boston. Photography thus becomes a starting point for advocacy relative to public policy and, in some direct cases, for new impulses for landscape architectural design.

In contemporary design circles, photographers have worked in tandem with designers to uncover landscape and urban issues and agendas that would help set paths for research and design investigation for years to come. Such collaborations have included Alex MacLean with James Corner in *Taking Measures Across the American Landscape* (1996, aerial photographs paired with map-drawings and texts on the underlying structures and logics of human-occupied landscapes across the continent), a project that has inspired a line of similar but deeper investigations into specific American geographies and attitudes toward landscape. These include Anuradha Mathur and Dilip daCunha's *Mississippi Floods: Designing a Shifting* Landscape (2001, the authors' own drawings, prints, and photographs on the various dynamic and engineered terrains along the Mississsippi River); Alan Berger's *Drossscape: Wasting Land in Urban America* (2007, the author's own drawings and photographs on brownfields and lastescapes of production and waste); and Richard Misrach and Kate Orff's *Petrochemical America* (2014, Misrach's haunting photographs and Orff's speculative drawings, both of the industrial landscapes of the petrochemical industry in the southeastern United States). I would also add to this mix (but in a parallel vein) Michael Maltzan's and Iwan Baan's collaboration in *No More Play* (2011), which poositioned Baan's photographs of common street scenes and urban landscapes in and around an evolving and maturing Los Angeles with transcribed interviews on the changing nature of urbanism and city life in the late twentieth and early twenty-first centuries.

But there's a deeper set of photographic roots here, tied directly to street photography and photography of the everyday landscape, depicted with the eyes of photojournalists and documentary photographers. The work of Jacob Riis and Lewis Wickes Hine, among others of this era, is very much in line with this tradition. Roy DeCarava, the first Black photographer to be honored with a Guggenheim

Foundation Fellowship in Photography in 1952, set his lens to capture the realities of everyday life on the street of Harlem in an effort that culminated in the publication of *The Sweet Flypaper of Life,* with a text by Langston Hughes, in 1955. In 1975, *New Topographics: Photographs of a Man-altered Landscape* presents works by ten photographers as art that "survey[s] the here and now" (from the catalogue)—or, as a visitor to the exhibit named Jack opined about the content of the photographs: "At first they're really stark nothing, but then you really look at it and it's just about the way things are." The work captures urban, suburban, industrial, and other altered landscapes across the US in black and white, very much a survey of the ordinary and unvarnished. Curator Britt Salvesen rightly aligned this photographic work with the almost contemporary work of those we now know as champions of the cultural landscape—J.B. Jackson, William Meining, Robert Venturi, and Denise Scott Brown. In a long era of social and cultural upheaval, in which so many sources of authority and custom were questioned and superceded, this new take on photography as stark depiction of the world *as it is* took its place as a recognized cannon of inquiry. It has become a touchstone for countless others like Mike Belleme, who introduced the work to me, and continues to extend and evolve today, with photographers such as Jules Allen in New York and Michelle Groskopf in Los Angeles bringing their own situated eyes and personal backgrounds and lived experiences to the world at hand.

A rediscovery of similar works in my own search for a collaborator proved meaningful and shed a similar light, but this time on life in big city urban parks and open spaces. According to *New York Times* journalist and editor Jim Dwyer, a series of photographs was commissioned in the height of New York City's financial ruin of the late 1970s and came just after a three-month newspaper strike; they never came to light until the *Times* published a selection of them in a special section on April 29, 2018 titled "Scenes Unseen: The Summer of '78." The initiative was part of the *Times'* effort to get its photographers back to work and came about thanks to an agreement with the City Parks Commission to capture public life at the end of the summer. What they saw is described by Dwyer:

Photos by Mike Belleme

> New Yorkers swarmed their parks, pools and beaches in 1978. They drank beer and licked Popsicles and smoked weed. They sunned themselves and they painted watercolors. They roasted entire pigs over pits of coals, and they soaked their feet in fountains beneath a steel globe 14 stories high. Big grown adult people double-dutched. Little ones squatted on haunches to go eyeball to eyeball with dogs. The city was a financial ruin and stuff was busted and it seemed it would be that way forever.... So people napped on rock slabs at beaches and tottered along piers so rickety-tilted that it was hard to see how everyone didn't slide right into the water. They broke bread, turned batter park benches into cathedrals.

In other words, New Yorkers improvised, they made these spaces their own. They became part of the vibrant afterlives of the city's parks in ways both anticipated and not—and were captured simply being themselves and interacting, creatively, with the people and world around them.

Like with this long line of photographers capturing the realities of urban life and urban landscapes, Mike Belleme's work struck me in a number of ways that resonated with our studio's approach to design and to the ways in which we observe, engage, and learn from people. I discovered his work in the Sunday *New York Times* in a photographic essay on Walmart parking lots in the American South, a collaboration with his friend and colleague George Etheredge. (It turns out that Walmart allows people to use their parking lots to sleep or camp overnight). After further research, I was especially taken with the often gritty, raw, and sometimes touching ways he captures life and landscape in an off-the-grid community in the mountains of North Carolina, a project he calls *Wild Roots.* Belleme's curatorial eye supersedes project, assignment, or politics—his work titled *Stars and Bars for Al-Jazeera* straightforwardly but pointedly portrays a Confederate rally in Knoxville as part of an assignment for a Middle Eastern news outlet, while he chronicles his own interests and relationships with skateboarding and skateboarders in a series of projects and portraits. Belleme's work is a straight yet empathetic presentation of people and scenes as they are, doing what they do—no gloss, no apologies. In so many ways, these are the people we deal with in our everyday work—multiple publics, multiple voices, doing what they do, being who they are. These are the folks who ultimately come to inform our work, and eventually may inhabit the landscapes and cities we design. They need to make them their own.

—

Mise-en-Scène sits squarely within each of these lineages. It is at once an artful documentary project on contemporary cities, city people, and the forces playing out across cities and public spaces everywhere. But it's also a creative project about the future, about identifying pathways forward; about how people as individuals and entire communities, with artists, planners, designers, thinkers, government leaders, citizens, and activists can collaboratively shape our futures. It celebrates what is distinct about each of the cities and the various people who live in them. It points to the commonalities that connect us all—those "social common denominators" (in artist and activist De Nichol's words) that we need to both survive and flourish—namely food, water, personal and environmental health, and meaningful social and personal interactions.

Mimi Zeiger's "On Edge" tackles the intertwined relationships of climate, economy, and social conditions in the city, using metropolitan and regional Los Angeles as a point of departure and the pandemic as a backdrop; Mimi's positioning touches on the often fraught psychological, social, and cultural circumstances of being on geographical, political, and environmental "edges." De Nichols expounds in different ways on the lines that are often drawn in cities—physical, economic, racial—and about the efficacy of social activism in cities such as St. Louis when lines are crossed and geographies and personal relationships are re-scripted. Julia Czerniak in "Appearance and (Aesthetic) Experience: The Ongoing Project of Stoss" speaks to the ways in which a design practice, working from the core of the discipline of landscape architecture, can take on an extraordinary and increasingly complex array of urban, social, and environmental agendas to begin to reshape the cities and environments that become stages for urban daily lives—with a larger cultural Project contributing equally to the work at hand. Nina-Marie Lister positions all of this within the pressing climate crisis of the twenty-first century by pointing to the need to find new ways of working collaboratively across boundaries, to engage and activate landscapes as critical infrastructures of resilience. Sara Zewde reflects on the nature of the image in the context of cities and social/intellectual agendas, and in relationship to design, offering the photographic lens and the designed space or artifact as ports for embodying the now and projecting new futures. Together, they highlight the tensions, the aspirations, and the very real concerns associated with changes taking place in cities and urban landscapes today.

—

This project was started before the pandemic of 2020 broke out—all the photographs were taken prior to COVID-19 shutting down cities around the world, and most of the drawings were being finished up. But it and the essays all came together in a radically re-made world, shaped in as-yet-untold ways by disease, violence against Blacks, protest, and political upheaval. In the end, the book will emerge in a world that could be more or less certain than the one in which I write from now. Some of it will persist, in one form or another. New acts to come, new scripts to write and to improvise—as has occurred over and over again for millenia.

Los Angeles, California

A sprawling metropolis on the edge of the continent, Los Angeles has been evolving, maturing, and reckoning with its precarious resources and vulnerability to wildfire, power shortages, and water supply. Its arid climate and legendary outdoor lifestyle belie pressing transportation, housing, and open space needs. An ethnically and culturally diverse mix of people moves about the expansive city grid, often struggling to find relief from the heat or from the racial and economic disparities that have become more and more stark. Yet life persists in surprising ways, and intimate moments occur in unexpected places.

San Fernando
Granada Hills
Lake View Terrace
Sunland Tujunga
Angeles National Forest
Chatsworth
Northridge
Canoga Park
Sun Valley
La Cañada Flintridge
Reseda
Van Nuys
Burbank
North Hollywood
Woodland Hills
Encino
Pasadena
alabasas
Glendale
Griffith Park
Northeast Los Angeles
Topanga State Park
West Hollywood
Frogtown
Silverlake
Westwood
Beverly Hills
Central LA
Brentwood
Chinatown
alibu
Pacific Palisades
Mid City
Downtown
Boyle Heights
Santa Monica
East Los Angeles
Culver City
Crenshaw
Venice
South Los Angeles
Inglewood
LAX
Downey
El Segundo
Compton
Pacific Ocean
Manhattan Beach
Lakewood
Torrance
Carson
Wilmington
Long Beach
Rancho Palos Verdes
Terminal Island
San Pedro

WEDBUSH

SPORTS • TOYS
• BEACH TOWEL
• REDBULL
BATTERIES
CIGARS
ATM
Max withdraw
Max
withdraw
$200
ATM
Hot Dogs
Lycamobile
GONZO

Cobbled together out of swamp, floodplain, desert, and mountains, short of water and painfully dependent on far-away resources to survive, Los Angeles is sited on inhospitable terrain, located where the continent runs out of land. No city should be here.

Kazys Varnelis

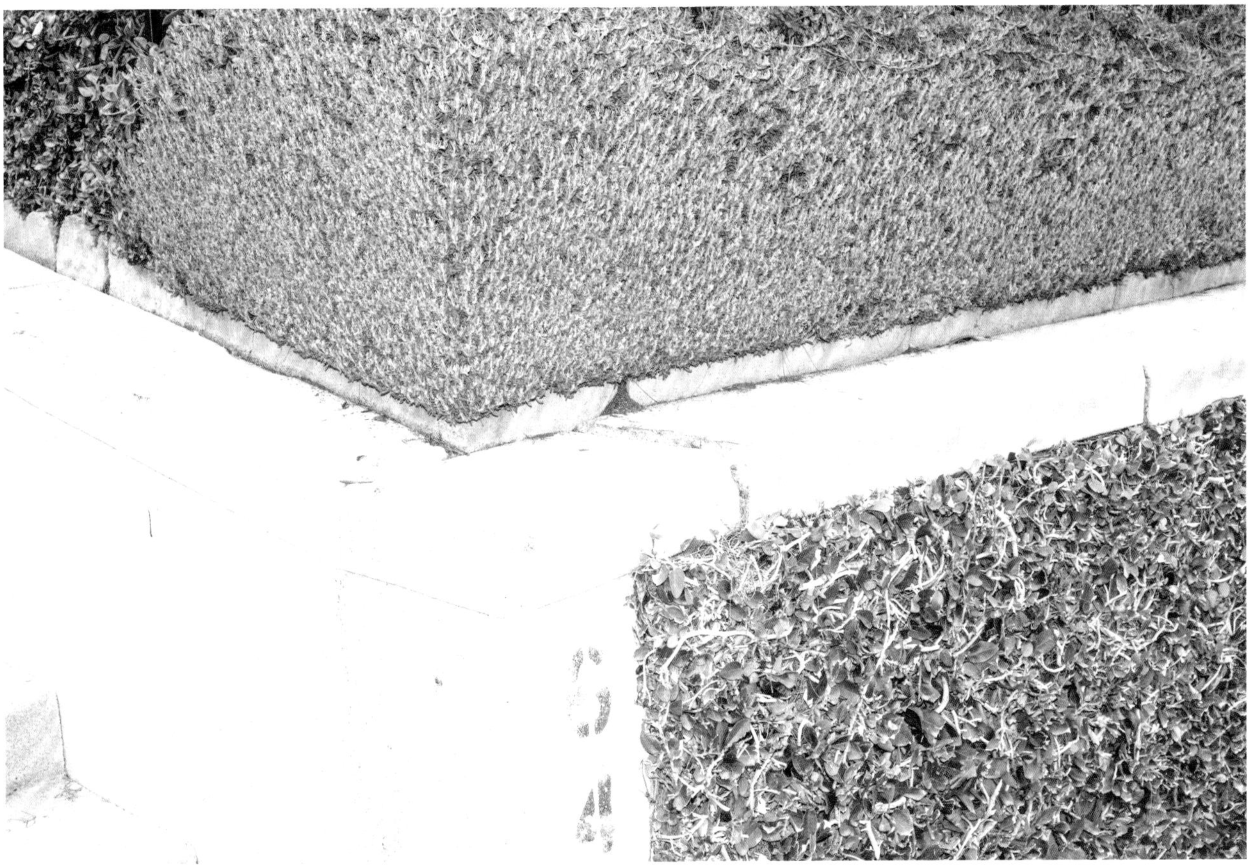

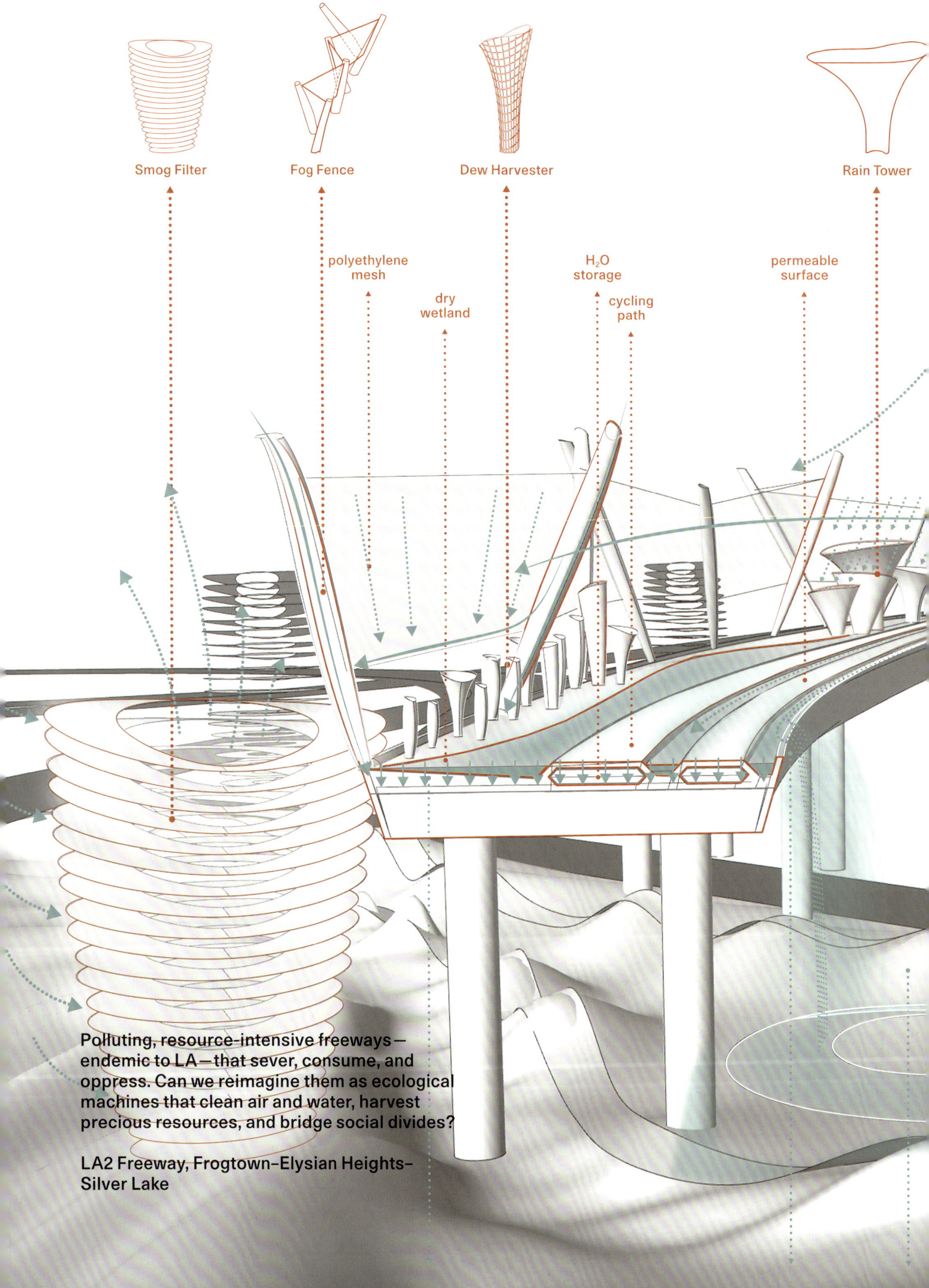

Polluting, resource-intensive freeways—endemic to LA—that sever, consume, and oppress. Can we reimagine them as ecological machines that clean air and water, harvest precious resources, and bridge social divides?

LA2 Freeway, Frogtown–Elysian Heights–Silver Lake

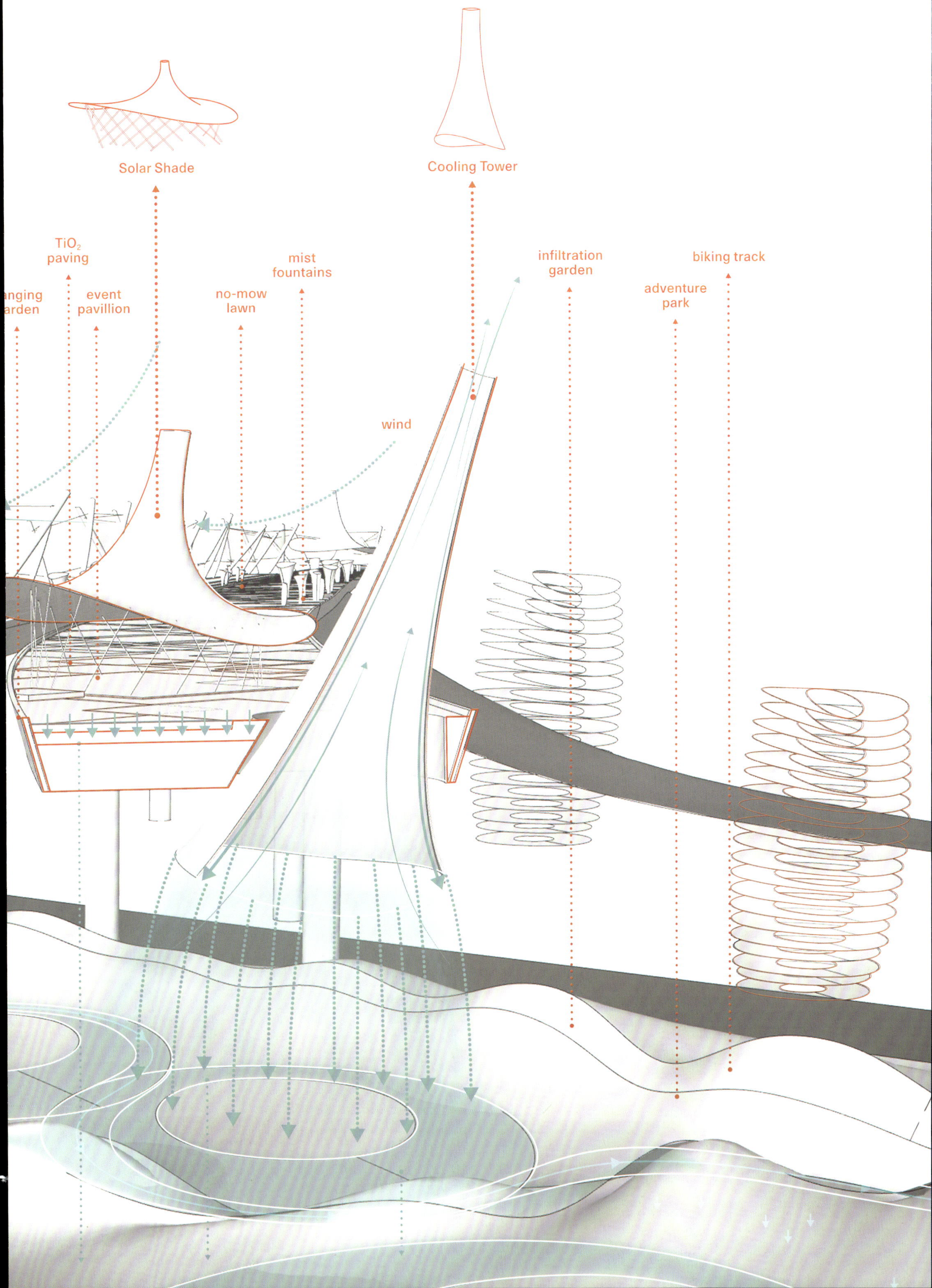

Solar Shade
Cooling Tower
TiO2 paving
anging arden
event pavillion
no-mow lawn
mist fountains
infiltration garden
biking track
adventure park
wind

What was construed by people in the rest of the country as accidental—the sprawl of the city, the apparent absence of a cohesive center—was in fact purposeful, the scheme itself: this would be a new kind of city, one that would seem to have no finite limits, a literal cloud on the land that would eventually touch the Tehachapi range to the north and the Mexican border to the south, the San Bernardino Mountains to the east and the Pacific to the west; not just a city finally but its own nation, The Southland.

Joan Didion

LIFEGUARD
OFF-DUTY
911
KEEP OFF

Rotary Dr
1700 N
WARNING
NEIGHBORHOOD WATCH
WE LOOK OUT FOR EACH OTHER!
SLOW DOWN
SILVER LAKE
Since 1958
Post

Rotary Dr
1600
NO PARKING ANY TIME

LA is the land of constructs. While many real struggles exist within this complex city, just as many are fabricated by a society obsessed with perfection. The image of the sculpted round tree in a modest front yard speaks to the futility of this pursuit for most. The white picket fence, the universal symbol of middle-class assimilation, paint chipping from its surface. Shoots of new growth rebelliously defy the tended perfection of the manicured tree. Control and chaos in a constant struggle all reflecting our own self-worth and social standing for all the world to see.

Mike Belleme

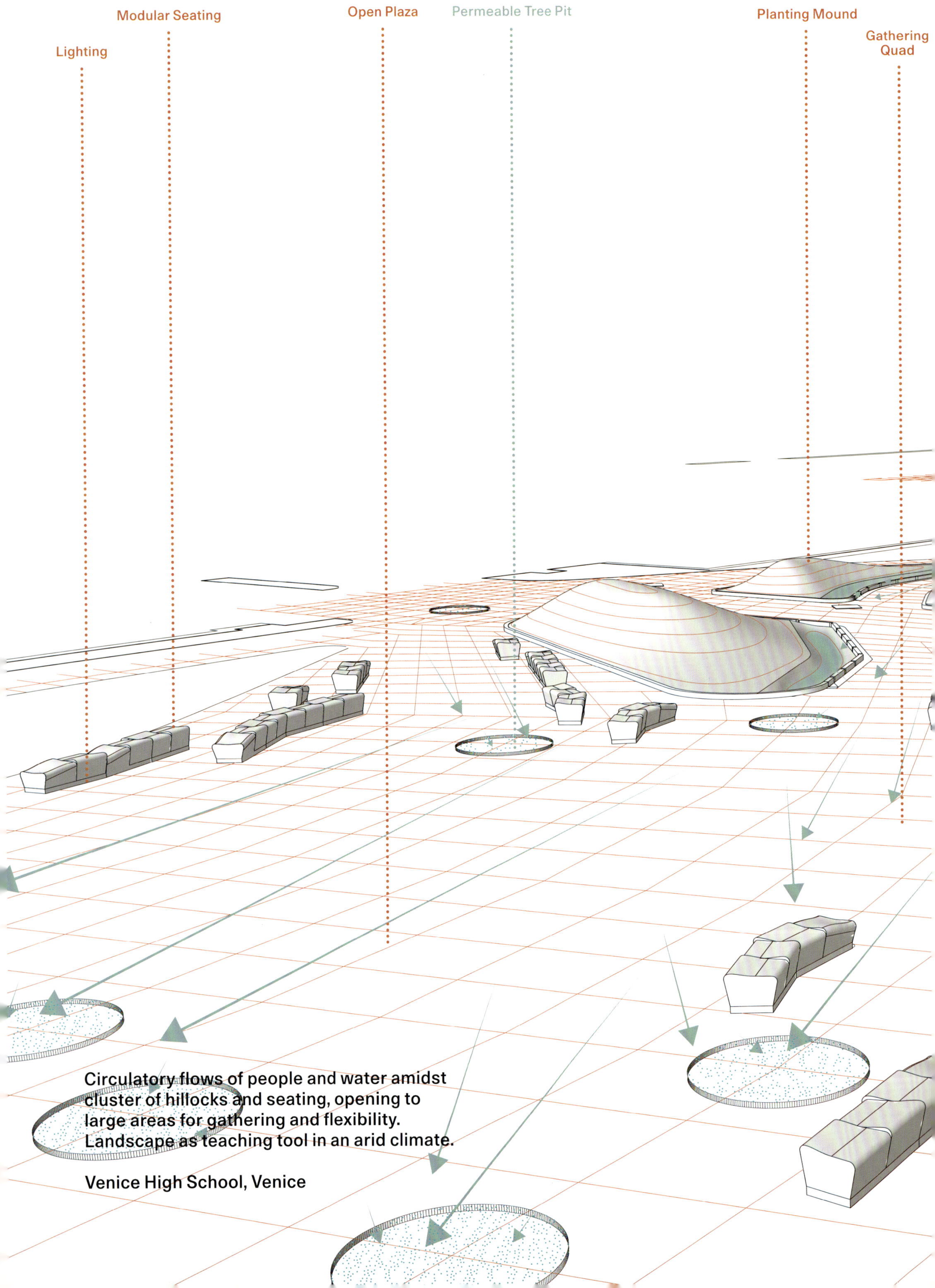

Circulatory flows of people and water amidst cluster of hillocks and seating, opening to large areas for gathering and flexibility. Landscape as teaching tool in an arid climate.

Venice High School, Venice

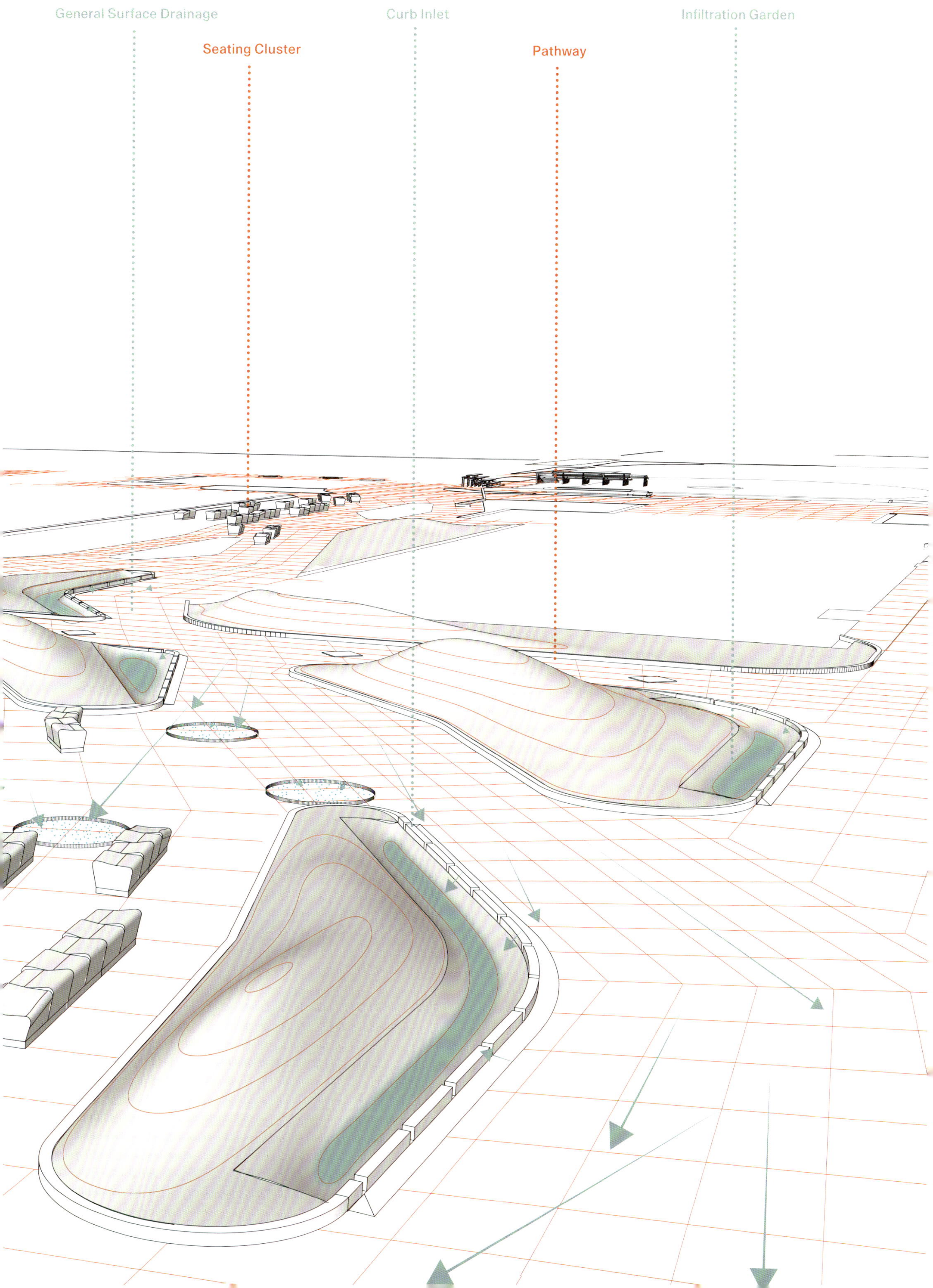
General Surface Drainage
Curb Inlet
Infiltration Garden
Seating Cluster
Pathway

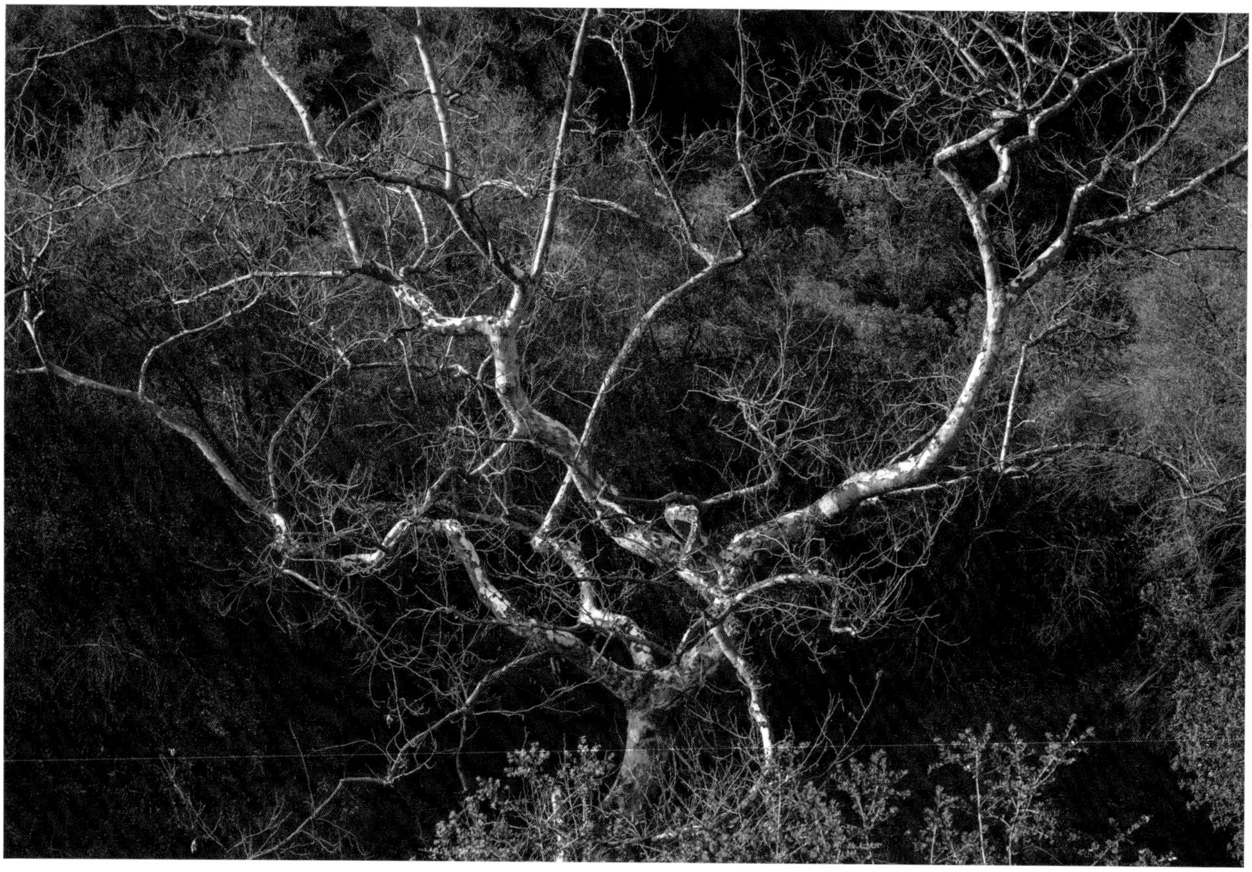

As much as any other city, Los Angeles is
a work-in-progress, a landscape of fragments
where the boundaries we take for granted
in other environments are not always clear.

David L. Ulin

On Edge

Mimi Zeiger

To us kids—most of us—the trip was just an adventure, an excuse to go outside the wall.

Octavia Butler[1]

This is a story of uneasy coexistence across elusive divides. Early on in the pandemic, I stopped walking my dog at night. Every morning I take long walks around Pasadena. Leaving my neighborhood with its condos and apartment buildings, an archive of the various stylistic trends in stucco from sixties mod to nineties Spanish Revival on steroids, I walk south, crossing an invisible zoning line between multifamily apartment buildings and single-family homes. Income and lifestyle change as I cross the line. On the other side are tightly edged lawns and meticulous rose gardens maintained by crews of Latino landscapers in broad straw hats and masked in bandanas. My little Yorkie barks ferociously at their leaf blowers while I, embarrassed, try to quell his tempest-in-a-teapot rage.

This daytime routine is a choreography of privilege—of my middle-aged, White body seamlessly crossing through irrigated landscapes and boundaries of class and policy. No one questions my movements. Some days, I pass the 1914 house that served as the governor's mansion for the 1980s sitcom *Benson*, that show in which Black actor Robert Guillaume played a butler to a rich, white family. It's a 16,000-square-foot, Classical Revival style manse with white columns worthy of Monticello.

Pasadena's urban fabric was shaped by exclusionary covenants and is still haunted by the racist strategies employed by developers and homeowners' associations, which persisted throughout the early and mid-twentieth century. Language in deeds kept "non-Caucasian" people from purchasing property within much of the city, despite being ruled unconstitutional by the Supreme Court in 1948. There's a neighborhood crime watch sign attached to the lamppost on the corner. The eye logo, a white teardrop shape on a police-blue background with a beady, black iris is ominous or omniscient, depending on the color of your skin. This ghost doesn't frighten me at night. I'm lucky in that respect. Luckier than too many Black and Brown people whose lives are cut short by those in blue.

The quiet puts me on edge.

When Los Angeles County ordered a curfew to try to quell protest and unrest, the only sounds were the beats of helicopter blades and hissing sprinklers. Metal birds illuminated by a huge waxing gibbous moon. A dozen miles away in Downtown Los Angeles, the hiss came from tear gas canisters. But in Pasadena, the streets were even more still than usual.

With most Los Angeles County residents staying at home, nights became the domain of other creatures. Flocks of wild parrots flew from palm tree to palm tree, their chatter the sound of dawn. Occasionally, I heard (or thought I heard) coyotes. Just like Joan Didion hears "occasional coyotes" in her 1965 essay, "On Morality," first written for *The American Scholar*.[2] Her coyotes are coyotes, but also symbols of skulking immoralities lurking in the dark. "Sinister hysteria in the air," she wrote in her meditation on conscience, what we now call virtue signaling, and the social codes governing the boundaries between right and wrong.[3]

My coyotes are coyotes. Reporting on the phenomenon of urban wildlife has been growing for years. A 2016 report from *Landscape and Urban Planning* noted that 90 percent of U.S. cities have coyote populations.[4] A more recent study by the National Park Service found that they feed mostly on domestic cats.[5] (I'm concerned about one licking his chops over my little Yorkie.) Los Angeles is one of two cities globally that have mountain lions within the metropolis. Big cats fascinate Angelenos, who track the movements of RFID-tagged cats named P-1 through P-80 with the same devotion as paparazzi hunting Kardashians. There's a motion sensor camera installed in Griffith Park that captures feline selfies. These pumas live in the Santa Monica Mountains, the dramatic range that frames the L.A. skyline, sometimes venturing into backyards under the Hollywood sign to feed.

In *Los Angeles, The Architecture of Four Ecologies* (1971), Reyner Banham dubbed this zone where pumas meet residential neighborhoods: Foothills. He describes them as "narrow, tortuous residential roads serving precipitous house-plots that often back up directly on unimproved wilderness."[6] Banham is less interested in the symbiosis between humans and nature and more in mapping economic and technological factors, leading to a celebration of John Lautner's cinematic Chemosphere—a lollypop house on a concrete stick—and a critique of intrusive "mountain cropping" for hillside development. "The financial and topographical contours correspond almost exactly: the higher the ground the higher the income," writes Banham.[7]

Five decades later, Banham's careful observations smack of anthropocentric concerns: the structural prowess required to build on steep land and concern that mother nature might eventually fight back. "Naturally one regrets the disappearance of Southern California's attractively half-tamed wilderness, but short of a social revolution or a major economic disaster they were going to get built on anyhow," he writes, a little too glibly. "The worry is that these extensive human settlements have been constructed on sands that have been shifted once by an outside agency, and may decide to shift for themselves at any time."[8]

We are living through another social revolution and a major economic disaster. Any edge between urban fabric and what we used to call wilderness is edge only in name. All but the steepest, least desirable hillsides

have been filled. John McPhee, in his environmentalist reporting for *The New Yorker* writes, "In Los Angeles versus the San Gabriel Mountains, it is not always clear which side is losing."[9] His phrasing emphasizes that between urban fabric and wilderness, it is a zero-sum game. It's not that it is rigged, there's just no way to win.

Losers spread out across the Los Angeles Basin—down the hill and past the 210 and 10 Freeways. When McPhee describes infrastructural debris basins tucked into the foothills and their impact in protecting downstream flows, he also recounts the burdens placed on majority Black, Latino, and Asian neighborhoods. "People of Gardena, Inglewood, and Watts no less than Azusa and Altadena pay for the defense of the mountain front, the rationale being that debris trapped near its source will not move down and choke the channels of the inner city, causing urban floods," he writes.[10]

Pasadena backs into the San Gabriel Mountains. There are walking trails that snake into the hills behind the NASA Jet Propulsion Laboratory. Oaks and laurels provide intermittent shade. Pussy willows grow along the creek. Veer from the dirt trail, and you'll find signs of active and abandoned homeless encampments tucked in amid the poison oak and long grass. A tarp half-hidden by branches, strewn cardboard, a neat pile of trash.

It's as convenient to think of cities as sprawl—endless growth encroaching stopped only by geographic limits—as it is to think of them as series of edges—freeways, railroads, waterfronts, or rivers. And we know that both characterizations hold true, marked by interspecies networks of co-dependence. Thick, intersectional zones are contested territories and repositories of cultural bias and the societal problems that we can't seem to solve.

In December 2017, the Skirball Fire burned through the neighborhood of Bel Air. City officials blamed the source of wildfire on a cooking fire in a homeless encampment.[11] A crisis of nature pegged to Los Angeles County's escalating housing shortage and an inability to provide shelter to its most precarious residents. The flames ignited dry grasses and chaparral along the 405 Freeway. Known as the Sepulveda Pass, that stretch of multilane asphalt cuts through the Santa Monica Mountains, connecting the LA Basin to the San Fernando Valley. Endowed institutions—the Skirball Cultural Center and the Getty Center—flank slopes to the west and Bel Air residences to the east. The

camp was hidden in a canyon to the side of the freeway. Out of sight, out of mind.

News photographs of the fire showed bright orange flames racing up hillsides toward sprawling mansions. Seven hundred residences were evacuated. "The fire was burning in the same general area as the devastating Bel Air Fire of 1961," wrote Susan C. Schena of *The Patch*.[12] "That blaze destroyed about 500 homes and led to various policy changes, including a prohibition on wood-shingle roofs and the strict requirement to remove brush from around properties." Her reporting suggests the ways municipalities and individuals spatialize and harden defenses.

Didion, with her innate ability to capture cultural anxiety, considers fire season more an atmosphere with an emotional edge than a line. "This is fire season in Los Angeles, and it has been a particularly early and bad one," she wrote in 1989. "Most years it is September or October before the Santa Ana winds start blowing down through the passes, and the relative humidity drops to figures like 7 or 6 or 3%, and the bougainvillea starts rattling in the driveway, and people start watching the horizon for smoke and tuning in to another of those extreme local possibilities—in this instance, that of imminent devastation."[13] She writes of acres burned and boxes of snapshots by the door. Just in case.

But maybe such seasonal neurosis is a benefit for those who can afford it. Just like shelter and security in our economically perilous age. In 2019, a brush fire ignited on opposite side of the 405 Freeway. As it burned toward the Getty Center perched high on the hill, Angelenos feared for the precious artworks and artifacts inside. Institution officials issued statements assuring everyone that the museum's design and landscape would keep the treasures safe.[14] Limestone façades. Saturated lawns. High-performance ventilation systems poised to suck the oxygen from all the galleries.

Brentwood, the neighborhood behind the fortified museum, was evacuated at 3am. Owners left their expensive homes in a rush, failing to notify their housekeepers and gardeners. Writing for the *Los Angeles Times*, Brittny Mejia interviewed immigrants from Guatemala and Mexico who had turned up for work, walking through smoky streets and passing police checkpoints. They found their employers gone, houses empty, and ash raining down. They worried about losing their jobs, about losing money from a day of work.[15]

Invisible boundaries are insidious: the race and class divides left by

redlining, limits of school districts bounding off "good" neighborhoods from "bad," voting districts, beach access paths, and public transportation routes.

Writer Octavia Butler grew up in Pasadena, and the ghosts of this city live in her novels. Written in 1993, *The Parable of the Sower* is set in 2024 in a city not unlike her hometown. She paints a dystopia based on climate crisis and economic disparity that seems to anticipate our own. Gated communities are not just for the wealthy, they outline working- and middle-class neighborhoods as last ditch safety measures against the desperate indigent with no wall of their own.

Butler's protagonist is fifteen-year-old Lauren Olamina. Her neighborhood wall is three meters high and topped with broken glass. As conditions both inside and outside the wall erode, the novel illuminates both the limitations of walls as defenses and the need for symbolic value they provide: "We came home and wrapped our community wall around us and huddled in our illusions of security."[16] Butler's words echo politicians' patriotic idiom about wrapping oneself in the flag.

Los Angeles is a sanctuary city located four hours from the wall at the United States–Mexico border. Despite the distance, it is a *de facto* border town. Butler's protagonist recognizes the wall as a flimsy talisman that she cannot fully trust. Such ambivalence presages the paradoxes of global border walls written about by political theorist Wendy Brown: for every expression of fortification there are global flows and informal forces of resistance working to undermine the barrier.[17] In some cases, this means corporations pressuring governments to ease trade restrictions or issue more visas. In others, coyotes ferry immigrants through tunnels or across deadly borderlands. The concrete and steel are weaker than the bureaucratic, surveillance, and military armatures designed to toughen the divide.

Science fiction precepts tell us that the most critical speculations are grounded in the present. Butler hardens political edges and social divisions, which today go unseen, into ramparts. Early in the novel she describes the boundary from Lauren's point of view: "The neighborhood wall is a massive, looming presence nearby," writes Butler. "I see it as a crouching animal, perhaps about to spring, more threatening than protective."[18]

Maybe it's a mountain lion, I think. I remember that mama cat P-80 was captured after Woolsey Fire, deep

in the blackened burn area of the Santa Monica Mountains.

Notes

1 Butler, Octavia E. *Parable of the Sower*. Open Road Media, 2012.
2 Joan Didion, "On Morality," *Slouching Towards Bethlehem*, (New York: Farrar, Straus and Giroux, 1968), p.157.
3 Ibid.
4 Sharon A. Poessel, Eric M. Gese, and Julie K. Young, "Environmental Factors Influencing the Occurrence of Coyotes and Conflicts in Urban Areas", *Landscape and Urban Planning*, January 2017. Website accessed June 19, 2020. https://doi.org/10.1016/j.landurbplan.2016.05.022
5 Katharine Gammon, "High-cat Diet: Urban Coyotes Feast on Pets, Study Finds," *The Guardian*, April 12, 2019. Website accessed July 12, 2020. https://www.theguardian.com/environment/2019/apr/12/protect-your-pets-cats-make-up-one-fifth-of-coyotes-diet-in-los-angeles
6 Reyner Banham, Los Angeles: The Architecture of Four Ecologies (Berkeley, Calif.: University of California Press, 2001), p 81.
7 Ibid, p. 79.
8 Ibid, p. 91.
9 John McPhee, "Los Angeles against the Mountains," *The New Yorker*, September 26, 1988.
10 Ibid.
11 Alene Tchekmedyian, "Bel-Air Synagogue Sues L.A. Over Skirball Fire Sparked at Homeless Encampment," *Los Angeles Times*, August 23, 2018. Website accessed July 12, 2020. https://www.latimes.com/local/lanow/la-me-ln-skirball-fire-lawsuit-20180823-story.html
12 Susan C. Schena, "Getty Fire Destroys Bel-Air Homes," *Patch*, December 6, 2017. Website accessed July 12, 2020. https://patch.com/california/brentwood/fire-erupts-sepulveda-pass-near-getty-center
13 Joan Didion, "Letter from Los Angeles," *The New Yorker*, September 4, 1989. Website accessed July 12, 2020. https://www.newyorker.com/magazine/1989/09/04/letter-from-los-angeles-4
14 Ibid, Schena.
15 Brittny Mejia, "Getty Fire: Housekeepers and Gardeners Go to Work Despite the Flames," *Los Angeles Times*, October 28, 2019. Website accessed July 20, 2020. https://www.latimes.com/california/story/2019-10-28/getty-fire-housekeepers-arrive-to-work

16 Octavia E. Bulter. *Parable of the Sower*.

17 Wendy Brown, "Chapter 1: Waning Sovereignty, Walled Democracy," *Walled States, Waning Sovereignty*, (New York: Zone Books, 2010), p. 29.

18 Octavia E. Bulter. *Parable of the Sower*.

Galveston, Texas

A city on a barrier island along the Gulf of Mexico, Galveston is poised (again) to be blown or washed away. It's a tenacious place that has rebuilt itself many times, a whole town raised to protect against floods, that has even made folk art from toppled trees in genteel neighborhoods. But the middle class has been priced out—only the wealthy and the poor remain as residents. Workers travel in and out on a daily basis, a steady rhythm interrupted by the intermittent flows of tourists on and off cruise ships and well-heeled, seasonal transients bypassing the main town to reach vacation houses. What is Galveston's future?

Trinity Bay
East Bay
Galveston Bay
Goat Island
Texas City
La Marque
Hitchcock
Bayou Vista
Pelican Island
East End
Tiki Island
Midtown
Galveston Island
Brazoria National
Wildlife Refuge
West Bay
West End
Gulf of Mexico

America

It is an island on the Gulf and my gateway to birds, nature, and vistas.

We need to protect what little green space is left.

I'm concerned about constant flooding and loss.

Local Residents

01. Existing Condition

02. Grand Staircase

04. Skate Park

05. Rocky Shore

Brainstorm: can a single-minded seawall be rethought to offer opportunities for social life and emergent ecologies? Study models for public engagement.

Galveston Seawall, Central Galveston Island

03. Overlook

06. Access Ramp

worthy
the Lord
revealed

BUMP

H2O and water have become opposites; H2O is a social creation of modern times, a resource that is scarce and that calls for technical management. It is an observed fluid that has lost the ability to mirror the water of dreams. The city child has no opportunity to come in touch with living water. Water can no more be observed; it can only be imagined, by reflecting on an occasional drop or a humble puddle.

Ivan Illich

Immediately recognizing me as not local, not from here, he started in about the huge oak trees that used to shade the large yard in front of the bar where the annual rabbit stew contest is held. Hurricane Ike had taken them, and the loss could not be overstated.

Mike Belleme

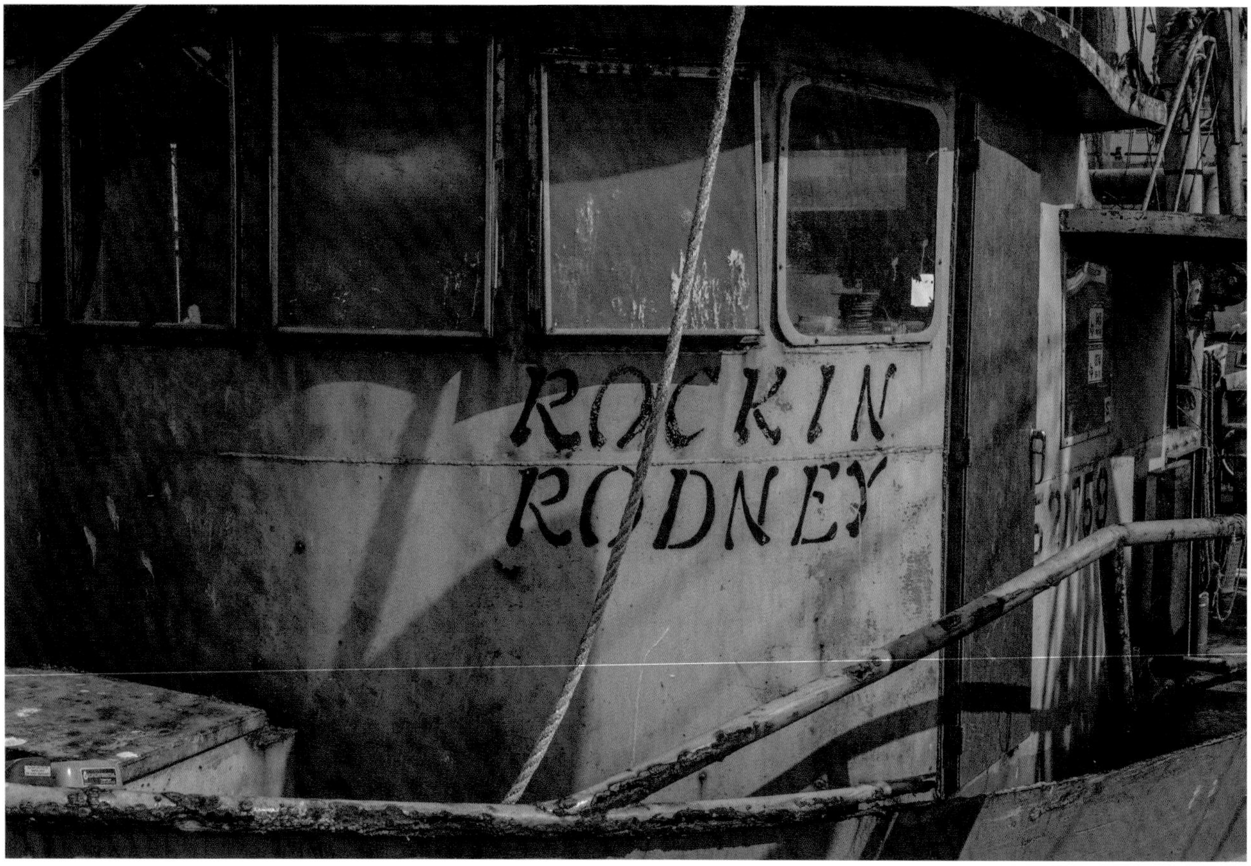
ROCKIN
RODNEY

BOAT
RAMP
AREA

Erosion, rising seas ... flooding. The cost of coastal insurance is pricing people out of Galveston.

Local Resident

How can Galveston economically survive and thrive? . . . erosion, storms, and subsidence. All things we can’t really control.

Local Resident

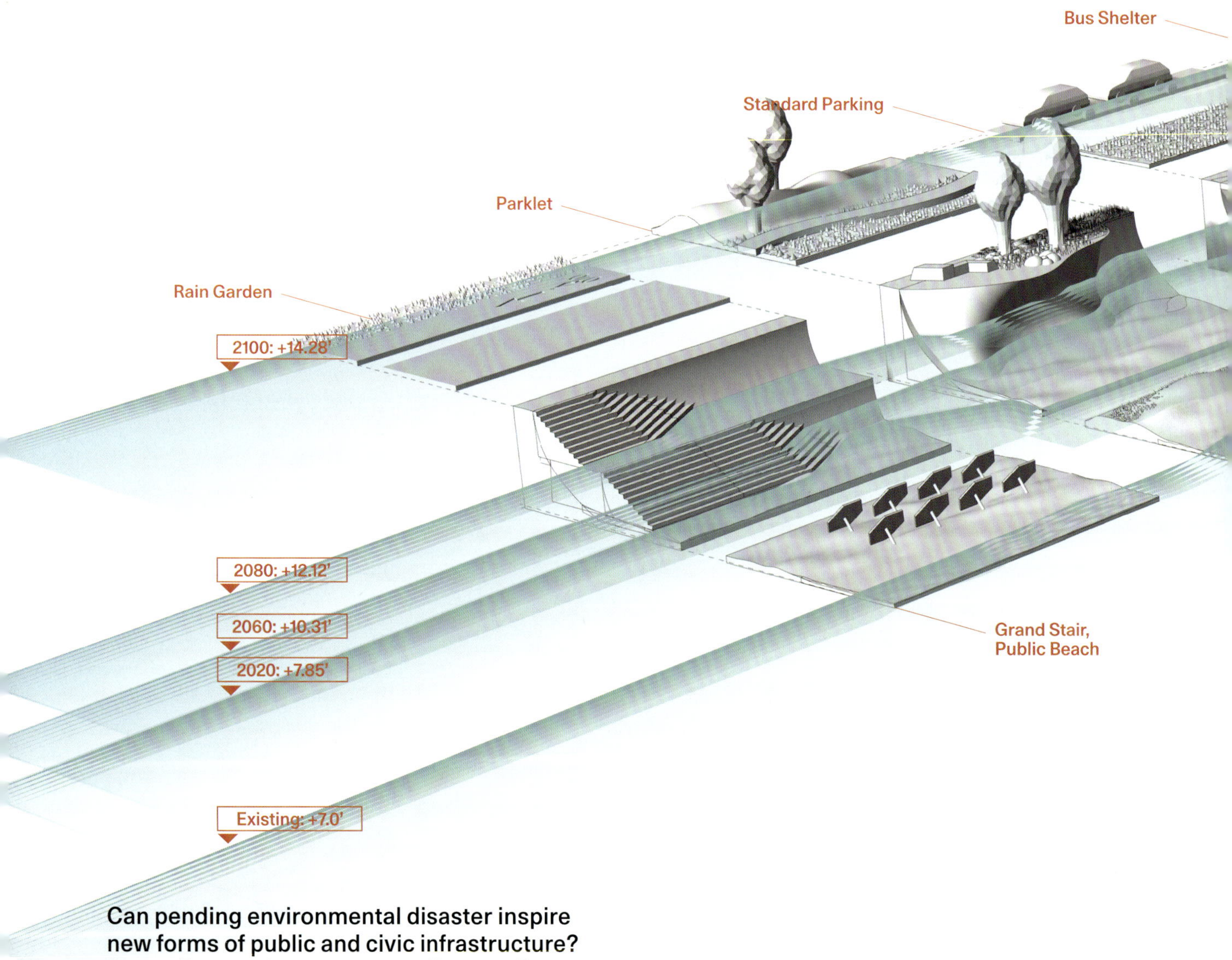

Can pending environmental disaster inspire new forms of public and civic infrastructure? Seawall upgrades to counter climate effects can inject new social activity, new adapted ecosystems: a social magnet at the beachfront.

Galveston Seawall, Central Galveston Island

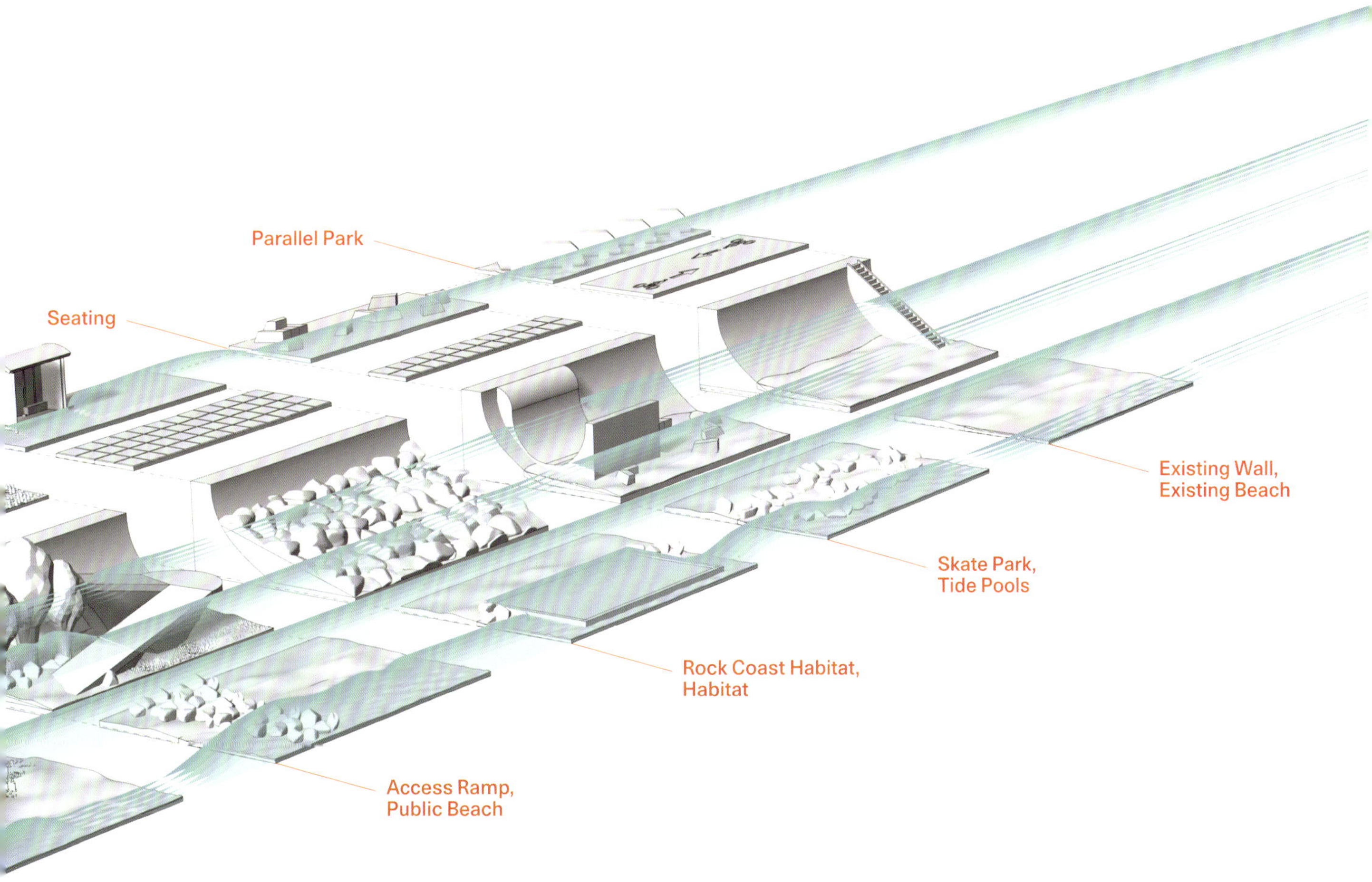

2100: Possible increase from Antarctic ice melt up to 7.87' total rise
2080: Possible sea level rise of 18" to 39" (1.5' to 3.25')
2060: To reach possibly 3' in this decade
EXT: Current water level is at 7'
1950" Sea level has risen 18" (1.5') between 1993 and 2018, the rate of change is 3.3mm (0.13") per year

KEY:
Year / Sea Level

Ext: +7.0'

Market
STOP
END
ROAD WORK

When you work with water, you have to know and respect it. When you labour to subdue it, you have to understand that one day it may rise up and turn all your labours to nothing. For what is water, which seeks to make all things level, which has no taste or colour of its own, but a liquid form of Nothing?

Graham Swift

EXIT
EXIT

St. Louis, Missouri

A culturally rich yet socially and racially challenged city at the center of the country, St. Louis is where the struggle for equal rights and for racial and economic equity continue to play themselves out in most visible and pointed ways. Many African Americans continue to live in poor neighborhoods that have not seen investment in decades, and the dividing lines (whether real or perceived) between neighborhoods as well as between Whites and Blacks, are sharp. This is a city looking to bridge and heal physical, social, racial, and economic rifts through ongoing dialogue, activism, and public realm initiatives. But it is always a work in progress.

Mississippi River
Florissant
Hazelwood
Ferguson
Chouteau Island
Normandy
Jennings
Maryland Heights
Gabaret Island
Chesterfield
Creve Coeur
Greater Ville
Fairground
Jeff Vanderlou
Clayton
Forest Park
Central West End
Old North
Richmond Heights
Gateway Arch Park
East St. Louis
Town and Country
Shaw
Downtown
Tower Grove Park
Affton
Lemay

Love Your Babies...
Born & Unborn.
Our Lady of Guadalupe for Life
Need Help?
1-800-712-HELP

NATIONAL

22ND JUDICIAL CIRC
OF MISSOURI

Color is not a human or a personal reality; it is a political reality. But this is a distinction so extremely hard to make that the West has not been able to make it yet. And at the center of this dreadful storm, this vast confusion, stand the black people of this nation, who must now share the fate of a nation that has never accepted them, to which they were brought in chains.

James Baldwin

A “city of islands” with a stark racial divide: a greenway attempts to reconnect people and communities, orient new approaches to social and racial equity, and forge new multi-racial futures.

Chouteau (now Brickline) Greenway Framework Plan

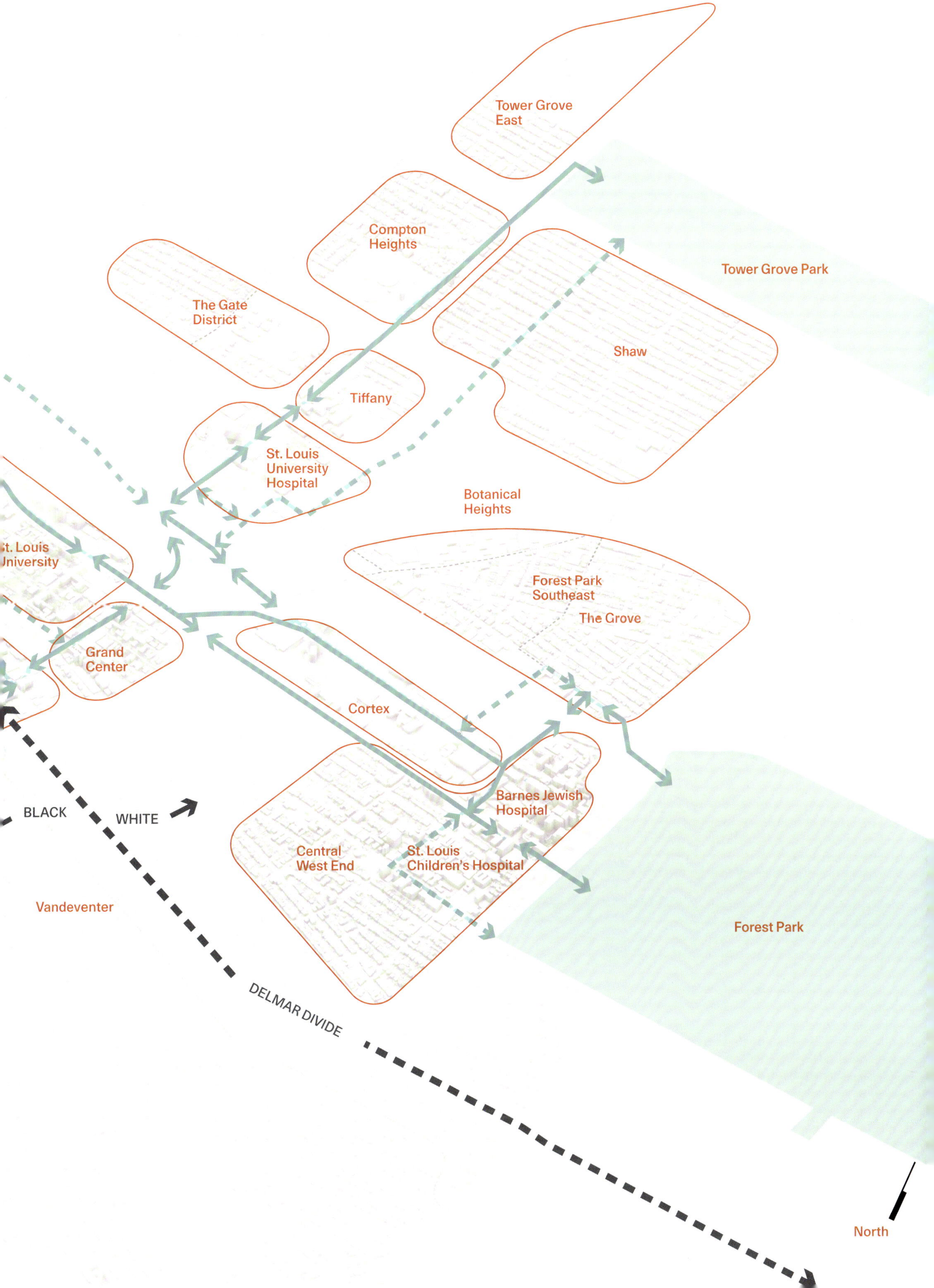
Tower Grove East
Compton Heights
Tower Grove Park
The Gate District
Shaw
Tiffany
St. Louis University Hospital
Botanical Heights
St. Louis University
Forest Park Southeast
The Grove
Grand Center
Cortex
Barnes Jewish Hospital
BLACK
WHITE
Central West End
St. Louis Children's Hospital
Vandeventer
Forest Park
DELMAR DIVIDE
North

Will look at the hair selection of the local drug store to assess whether 'they' want me here.

Local Resident

MR. MIKE POTATO

Kingshighway Blvd ¼
Hampton Ave 1¼
Clayton Rd 2½
TAYLOR
NEXT RIGHT

Budweiser

Three billion years of evolution have produced only one life form that can reverse this process [of plant colonization of land on Earth] and make our planet significantly less green. Urbanization is decolonizing the surfaces that plants painstakingly colonized four hundred million years ago, turning them back into hard and barren lands.

Hope Jahren

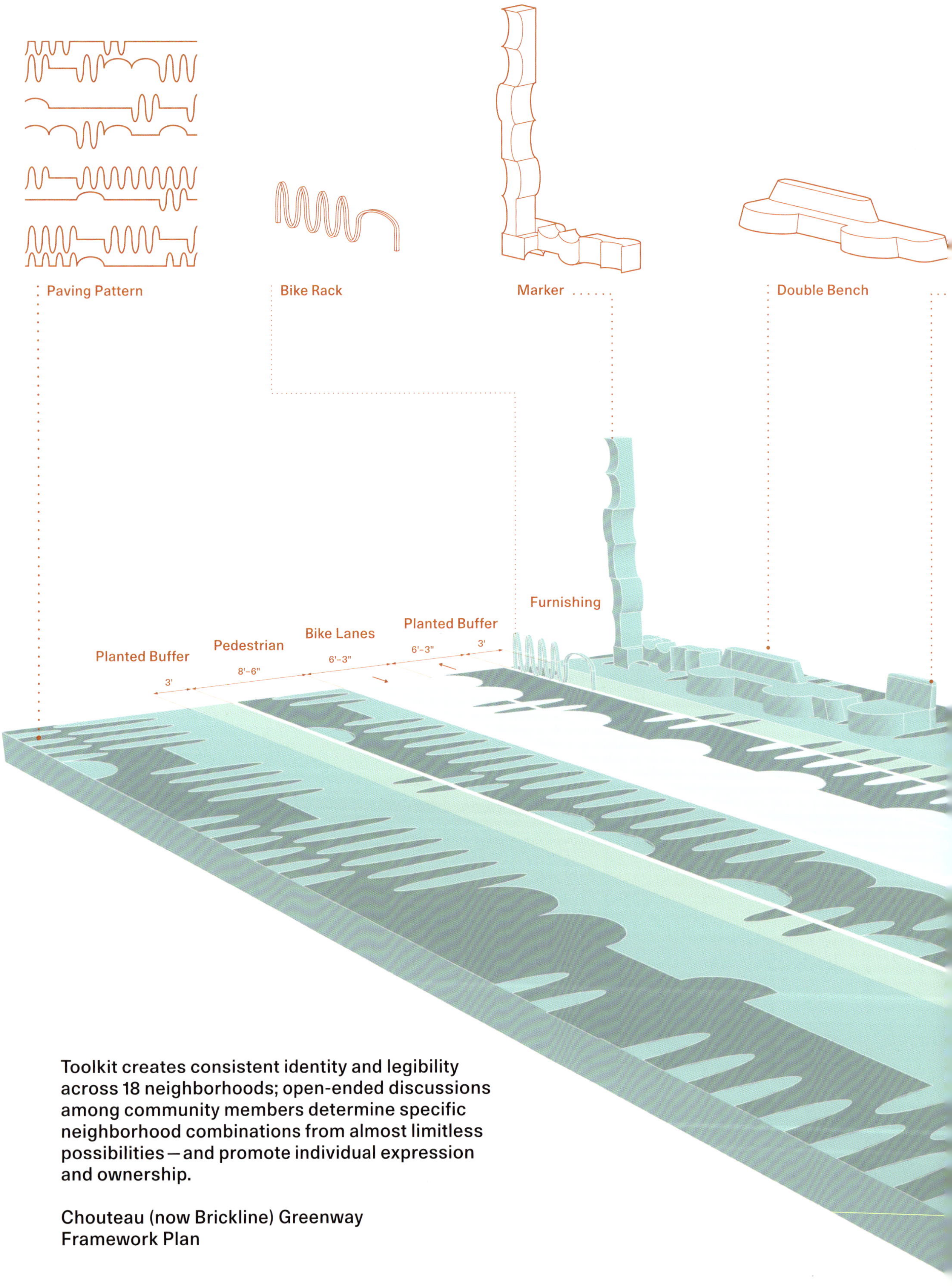

Toolkit creates consistent identity and legibility across 18 neighborhoods; open-ended discussions among community members determine specific neighborhood combinations from almost limitless possibilities—and promote individual expression and ownership.

Chouteau (now Brickline) Greenway Framework Plan

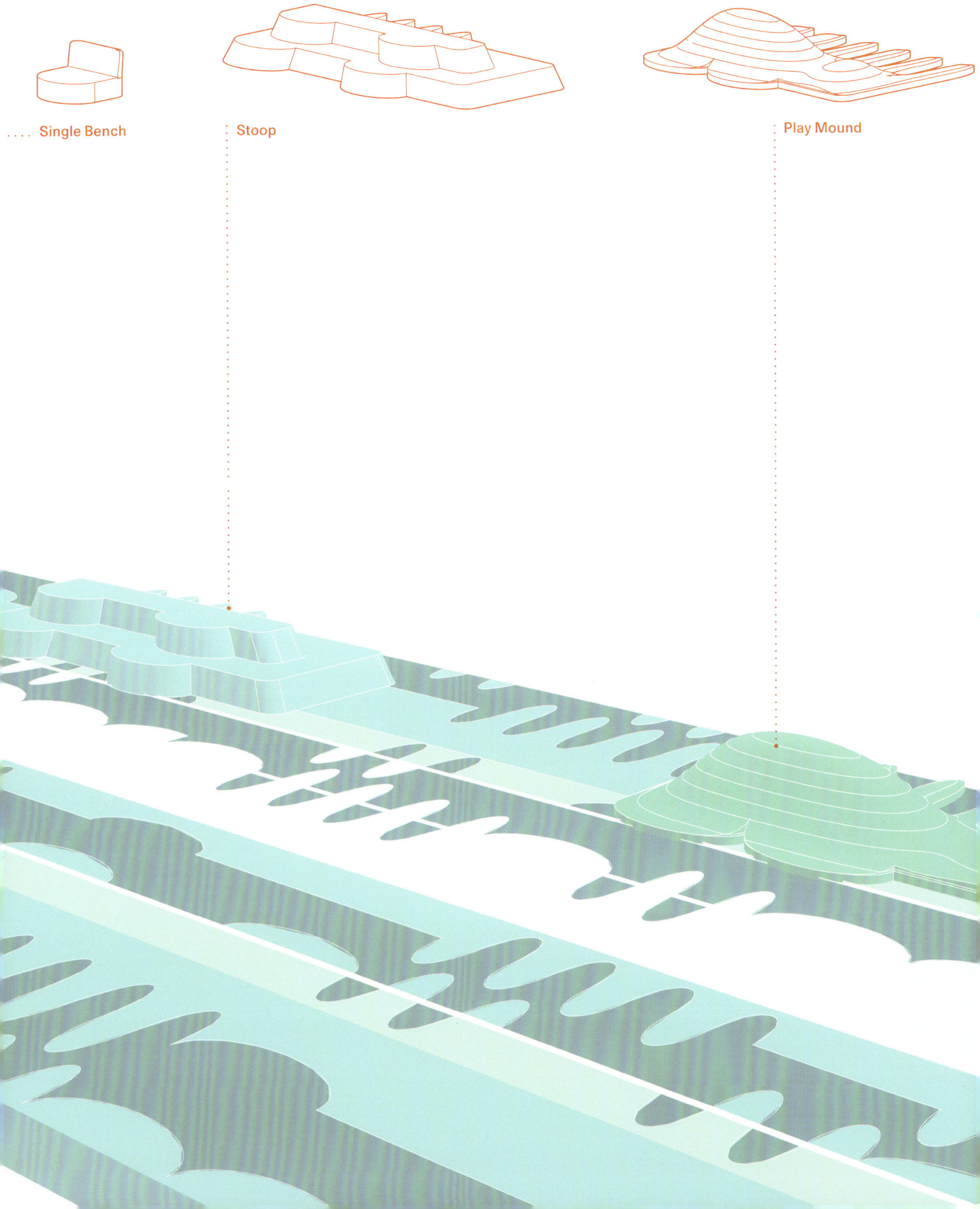
Single Bench
Stoop
Play Mound

Trust is broken and success is going to be
a heavy lift, but we can fix the problem.

Local Resident

Crossing the Line: Reflections of Spatial Activism in a City of Division

De Nichols

Race and identity ground the contexts of spatial divisions across American cities. Through structural and political exclusion and sociocultural dynamics that drive the migration and clustering of racial groups, most cities face continued challenges of segregation, gentrification, and marginalization of its residents.

I first learned and experienced such racial division as a child growing up in rural Mississippi in the 1990s. My hometown of Cleveland, MS, steadied Jim Crow's violent legacy of segregation through its downtown Cotton Row district and railroad track, which split the town into east and west. My family lived on the east side with other Black folks, but because my mom attended the local university and I was enrolled in the town's gifted program, I got to cross that dividing line to attend school, have my first campus experiences, and benefit from the bounty of resources that had been and were afforded to White students.

The western part of the town, with its manicured lawns and bushes in bloom, looked different from the east; it didn't have footpaths charted through people's yards as shortcuts to stores because its neighborhoods had sidewalks. The west side smelled different: the soul food and barbecue were the east side's aroma; the sounds, too, differed from the conversations, laughter, and 90's R & B music that filled our air.

I remember hearing my grandmother and her friends discuss the stories of Black families who courageously moved to that side of town only to have their homes burned down by White neighbors. During that time, I'd been significantly bullied at school by White school children who had already learned to target vitriol toward Black people who dared to claim space amongst them.

These memories remained with me when I moved north to St. Louis, MO, for college. It was there that I noticed a similar but amplified spatial segregation and racial fear sharing space with Black people. Cleveland seemed a microcosm of St. Louis, and yet the line of Cotton Row's railroad track I crossed to access quality primary education paled in comparison to the myriad physical and assumed racial lines that St. Louisans crossed or avoided. As a metropolitan region with 88 municipalities and a city of 79 neighborhoods, St. Louis exists as a quotidian exercise of crossing lines.

In St. Louis, the equivalent of Cleveland's Cotton Row is the "Delmar Divide." It produces and reveals stark disparities in life outcomes, wealth, education, criminality, and well-being among its Black and White citizens and its north and south communities. But Delmar Blvd is not the city's only dividing line. Long known for its nearly block-by-block hypersegregation, the city has other major streets such as Vandeventer, Grand, and Washington boulevards that shaped their own micro-divisions. When I served as a community engagement specialist for the city's contemporary art museum, for example, I canvassed neighborhoods within a one-mile radius of the museum by foot to learn the influences of families' participation in the arts district. So often, the challenges these predominantly Black neighborhoods express reflect both an unwillingness to walk across the traffic of Grand and Vandeventer and the social mistrustful belief that the

district's educational and cultural institutions treat them without dignity and belonging when they cross into those spaces.

Communities in both Cleveland and St. Louis attempt to atone for the violence and ills of segregation by centering and celebrating cultural assets and experiences that emerge from their troubled histories. In Cleveland, this manifests as a celebration of the Blues. In St. Louis, it is about touting the grit and resilience that makes the city so addictive to those who choose to live there. White people in Cleveland might cross the railroad and highway lines to eat at the east side's soul food restaurants, find a cheap mechanic, or go to the local hospital, whereas this is rarely the case for North—i.e. Black—St. Louis. People who enter the city for the museums, baseball games, conferences, and concerts so often go to their destination, without lingering, or eating, or venturing beyond the central neighborhoods and districts they deem safe. They dare not cross into the swaths of Black communities that were once plush and thriving: the physical cues of houses, storefronts, and yards signal that these areas only belonged to those whom they should forget, ignore, and disinherit.

Recognizing these norms of navigation, I became an activist and began to more deeply understand the connection between how hypersegregation within the built environment feeds the systemic wage, education, wellness, and policing gaps that exist across the region. It was activism—protesting, specifically—that helped me understand why an 18-year-old boy like Michael Brown Jr. would be murdered in his grandmother's neighborhood for jaywalking, by a White police officer like Darren Wilson who left him to lie dead on the street's pavement for four hours on the blistering Saturday afternoon before he was set to start college. The extrajudicial murders of Black people like Mike Brown expose the complex and compound ways that the built environment fuels inhumane racial injustice and inequity.

During the 2014 uprising that lasted for 400 days in Ferguson, MO, I walked the streets in protest more than I walked my own neighborhood or our local trails and parks. On numerous occasions, fellow protestors and I would make our way from the very spot where Michael Brown was shot on Canfield Drive to the police department 2.5 miles away on S. Florissant Road. We would trek to a host of churches, community centers, and vacant strip mall shops that had become the headquarters and

presumed safe zones of the movement. To navigate between some spaces of protests, we often left the main thoroughfares and walked across unbridged ditches, through neighborhoods, and along narrow footpaths where fences were overgrown with littered grass. There was one park, Forest Wood Park, along the route that allowed us to catch our breath during the hour-long marches, but with underkept amenities and few details designed into the landscape to welcome anyone to meander or sit; there was shade from the sun's heat. This park differed significantly from the luscious trees, pavilions, and benched pathways that shaded the Shaw neighborhood and Tower Grove Park we marched after another Black teenager, Vonderritt Myers, had been shot and killed by a neighborhood security guard two months after Michael Brown's murder. And, as we crossed boundaries to expand protests to the streets of downtown St. Louis, the Central West End business district, and suburbs like Ladue and Clayton, similar physical elements of their landscapes reminded me of the differences I'd witnessed on the west and east sides of Cleveland.

Mobilizing and marching through these varied grounds helped us see these places more intimately and remove the veils that covered their inequities. I was harassed by patrons at the most deluxe mall of the county. I was tear-gassed in one the neighborhoods most lauded for its diversity and safety, and many were arrested for peacefully protesting in the most upscale tourist areas. With this, we began to systematically think about addressing the inequitable policies and practices that catalyze the circumstances for divisions and injustices that endure. For many, policy work includes working on the Ferguson Commission report's 189 Calls to Action to ensure racial equity regionally. For others, it means ensuring our region cultivates and supports elected officials who commit to enhancing the city's collective well-being. And for others still, it means advocating for the abolition of carceral spaces through efforts such as the Close the Workhouse Campaign.

Protesting additionally shifted how I approached my contributions to the city as an artist and design practitioner. My team and I became more interested in how our work could bridge, weave, unite, and connect people across the dividing lines our protests expose. We are developing initiatives around what we deem as Common Cultural Denominators to set grounds for using culturally

universal life experiences like eating, aging, walking, and storytelling to generate public interventions in both the physical and social barriers. And it deepens our approach to work on regional planning projects and urban design. When I served as an artist and strategist for the development of a local greenway, I realized my experiences as a protestor and organizer could enhance everyone's understanding of the issues. Designers and urban planners had only visited, researched, and observed those places of division; they had not, as I had, crossed the lines and been there in defense of Black life, well-being, and space. That required demystifying and expanding the narratives for them, of what a place is and can be. Challenging our team to lean into a more profound knowledge of divided space helped us set priorities on areas that suffer the greatest inattention and disinvestment. In the process, we unearthed efforts to honor those who have made previous strides and continue that legacy of civic, cultural, and social commitment to progress.

Because of protesting, we can no longer avert our eyes and our attention away from the physical cues of these structural inequalities; spatialized activism offers a chance to shift and radicalize the vision we as designers have as we approach the design of cities. What shifts in seeing can unlock beyond sites and spaces: We begin to see ourselves and our roles with more purpose and dynamism. We begin to dismantle each other's fears and allow ourselves to navigate and explore its different parts. But more so, we begin to take more significant strides to manifest justice and equity as a public commitment to love every part of the city.

Green Bay, Wisconsin

At the confluence of the Fox River and Lake Michigan, the small city of Green Bay has been rediscovering its sense of community in part through new urban and riverfront development. Its working landscapes are still very much in reach and very much shape the character of the neighborhoods and of the river. Football, music, and public events infuse the city with sporadic energy, and yet these same spaces allow for interactions between a child and her parent, intimate conversation, simple pleasures. New civic and collective life is emerging as the town adapts to evolving economic and environmental realities.

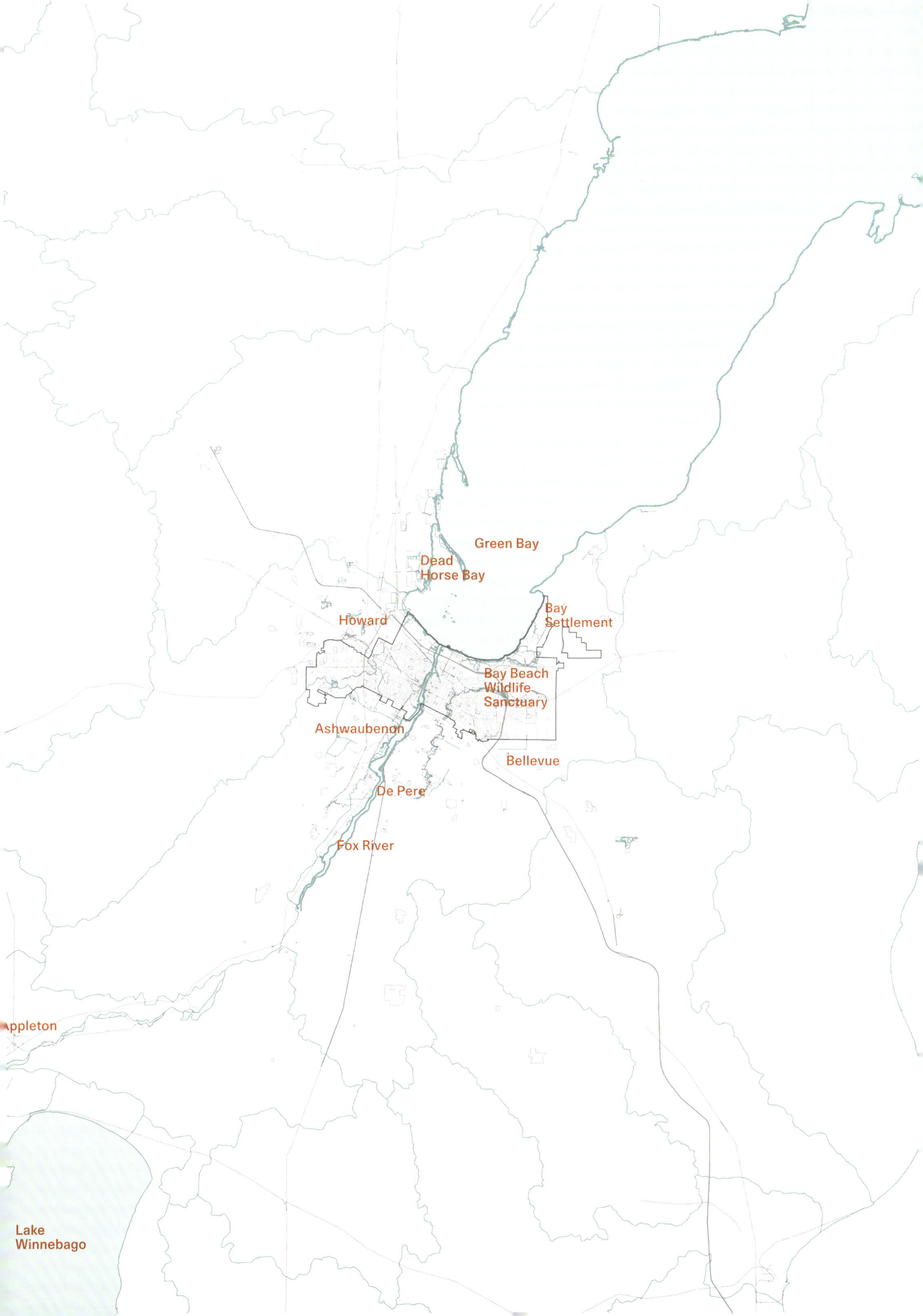
Green Bay
Dead Horse Bay
Howard
Bay Settlement
Bay Beach Wildlife Sanctuary
Ashwaubenon
Bellevue
De Pere
Fox River
Appleton
Lake Winnebago

TITLETOWN
TITLETOWN BREWING CO

TITLETOWN BREWING
7470
7470
7470
UNION PACIFIC
UNION PACIFIC
BUILDING

The industries were there because of the river. They had come for its navigational convenience and its fresh water. They would not, and could not, linger beside a tidal creek. For nature to take its course was simply unthinkable.

John McPhee

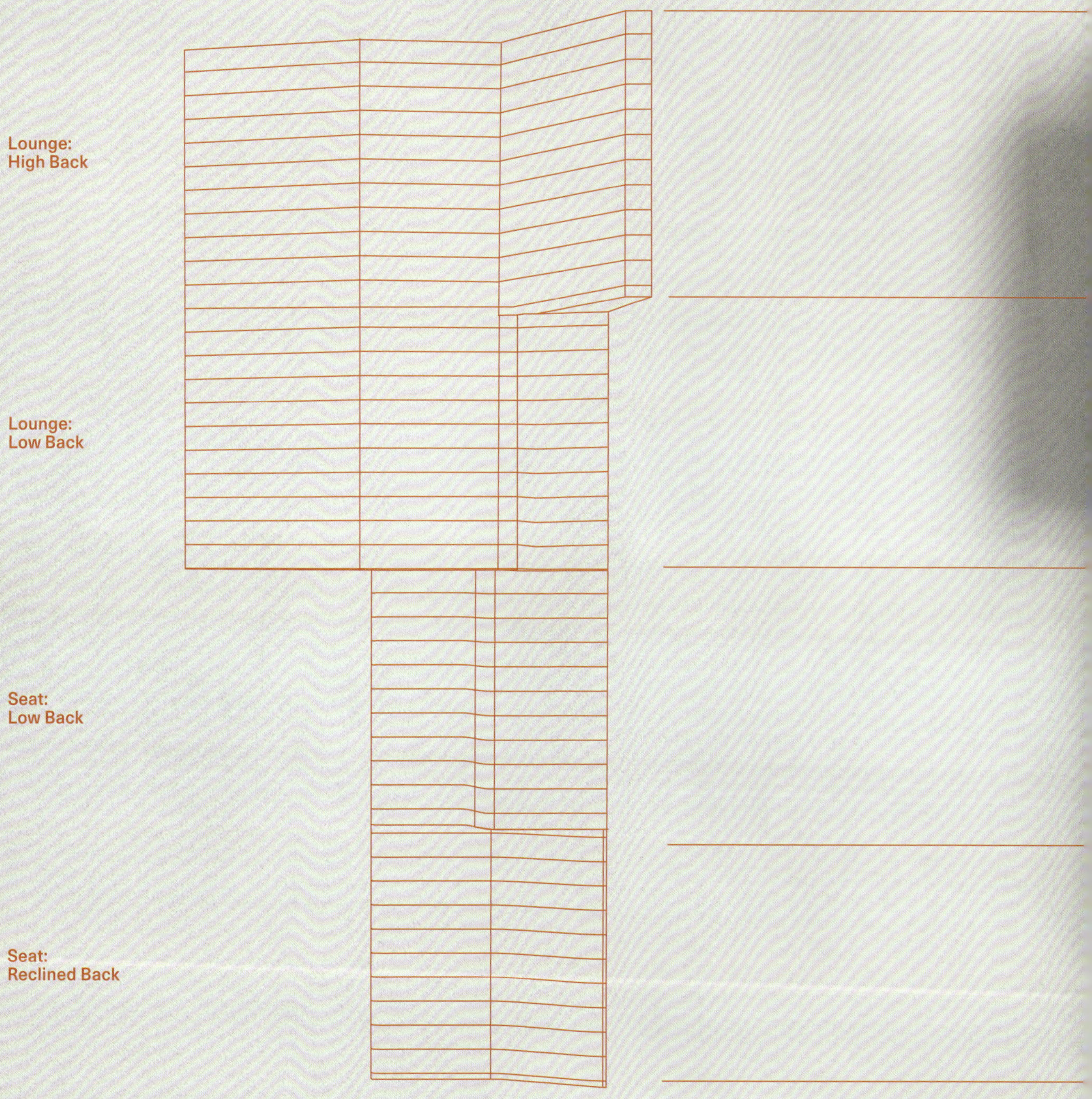

Wooden Origami 1: simple folds and inflections of a taut wood surface yield seating diversity, choices, difference.

CityDeck

HARO

ADAMS
17

Taste the Love
CULBY'S
CULBY'S
CULBY'S

The stage is set. Things seem to be prepared in advance for cameos, and even the sun is rigged like the expert lighting of a technician. The boundary between things and props is now dissolved, and the images of things have become things themselves. Perhaps the artificer's gold paint is still wet on such scenes in which we play at kings. Wandering around, I find this theatricality of the city life especially visible at the edges: the sleeping docks, the decrepit industries, the disused railroads: at such places, the city is shorn of all superfluity and reduced to its essentials, as in a play by Beckett. Flutes! Drums! Let the players in.

Teju Cole

PUBLIC
RESTROOMS

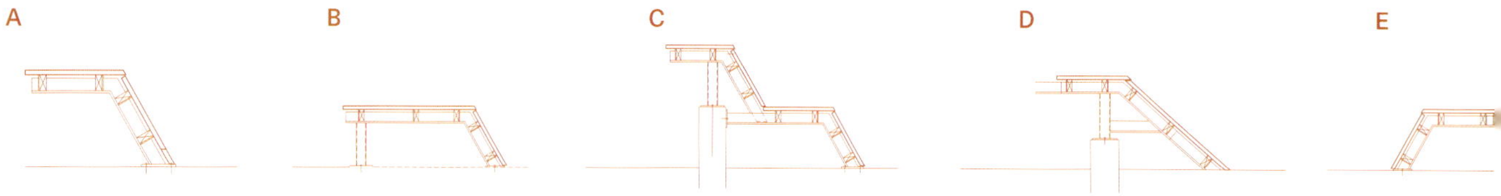
A
B
C
D
E

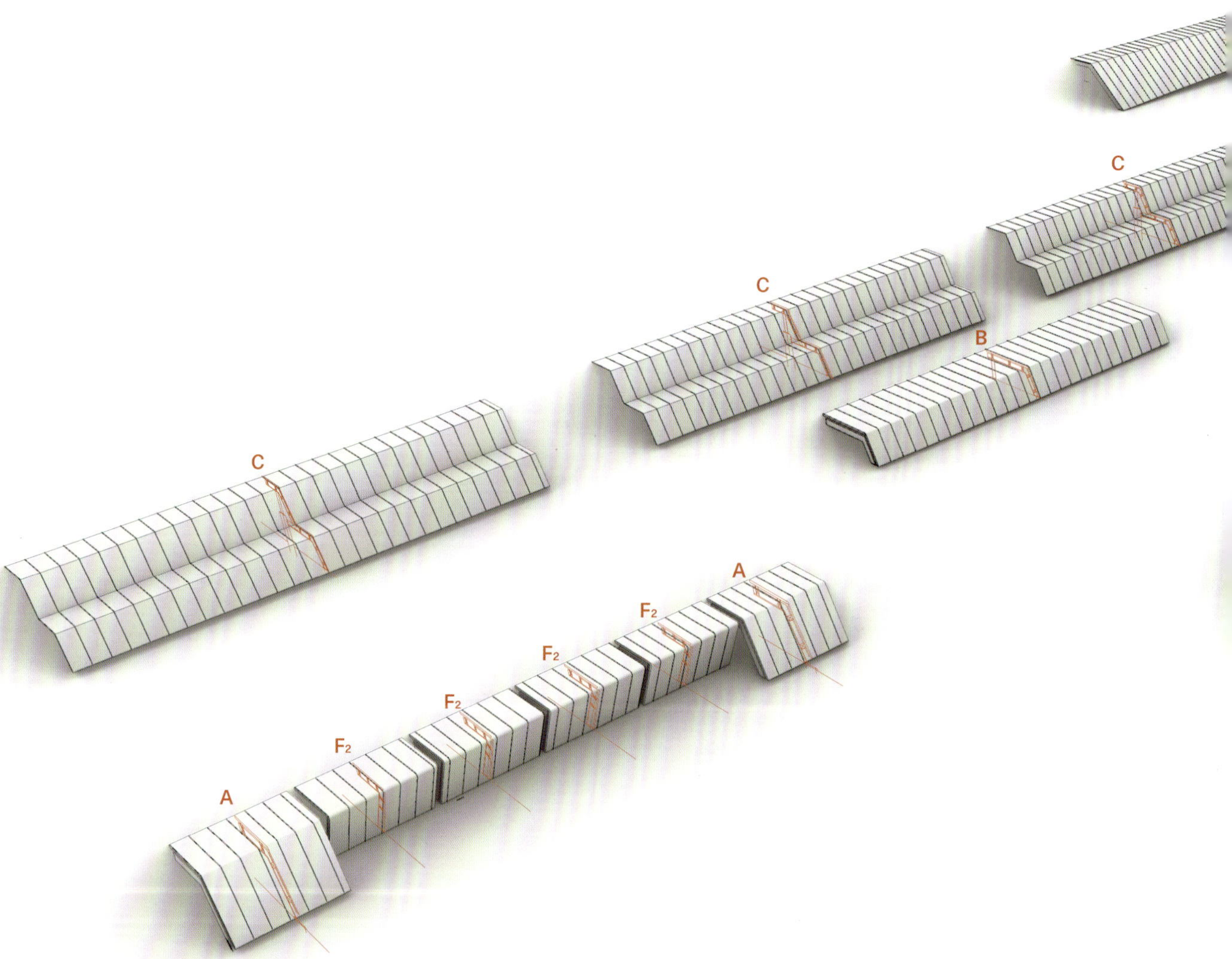
C
C
C
B
A
F2
F2
F2
F2
A

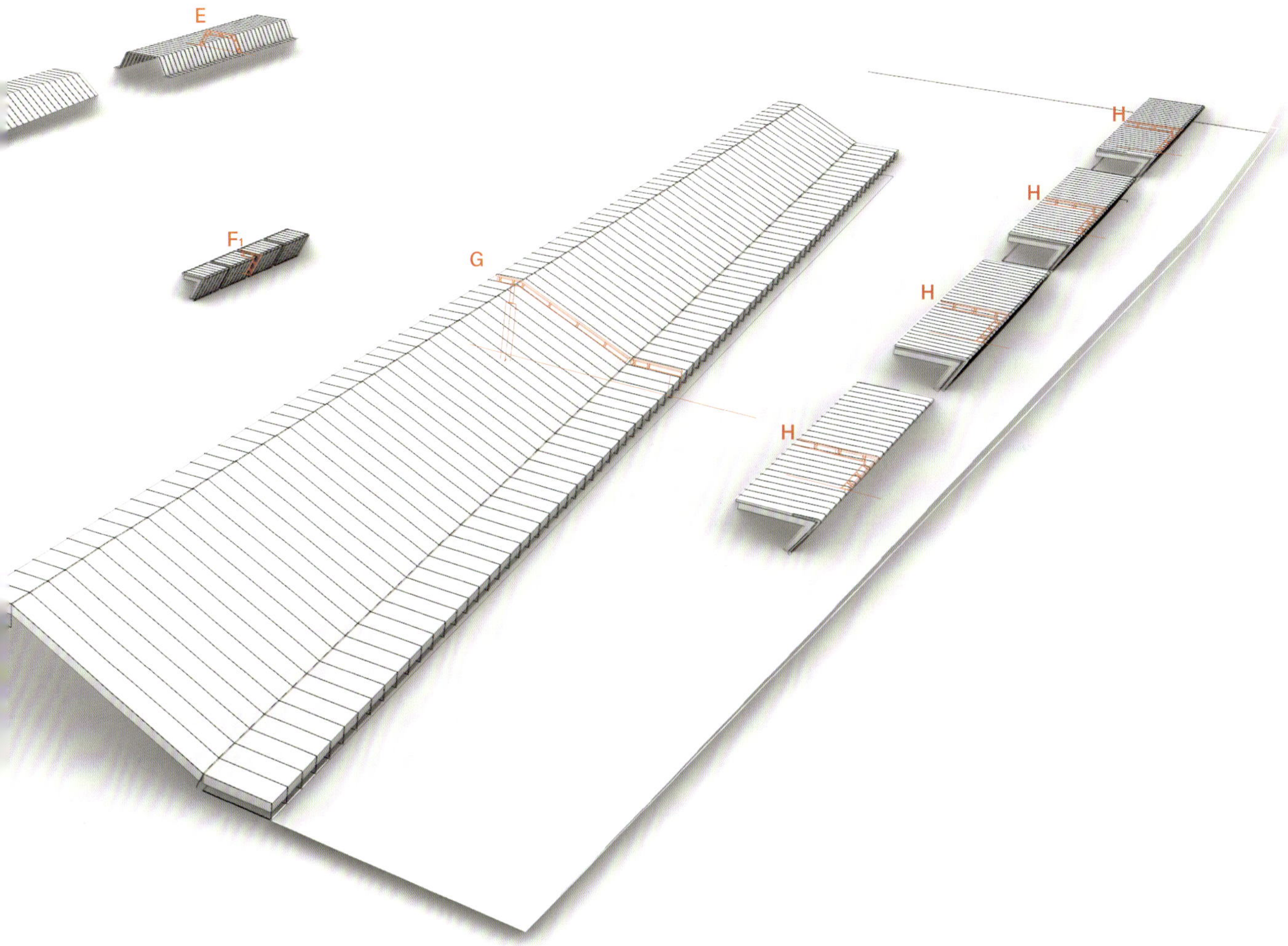

Wooden Origami 2: folded surfaces scaled to the human body and varied social groupings and to the forces and scale of the river.

CityDeck

THE
HABERDASHER

Ann Arbor, Michigan

A classic Midwestern university town set in an expansive landscape of rivers and ponds, of farming and woodlots, Ann Arbor is both a tight-knit community and a bustling academic center. Its energies ebb and flow with the academic calendar. Thousands of students and researchers mix regularly with locals throughout the school year, and respite comes during hot summer days. Access to nature beyond the center of town and campus is readily at hand, but nature and campus life often don't mix . Both improvised and designed landscapes offer opportunities for exposure to sun and to nature as well as for social interactions, large and small.

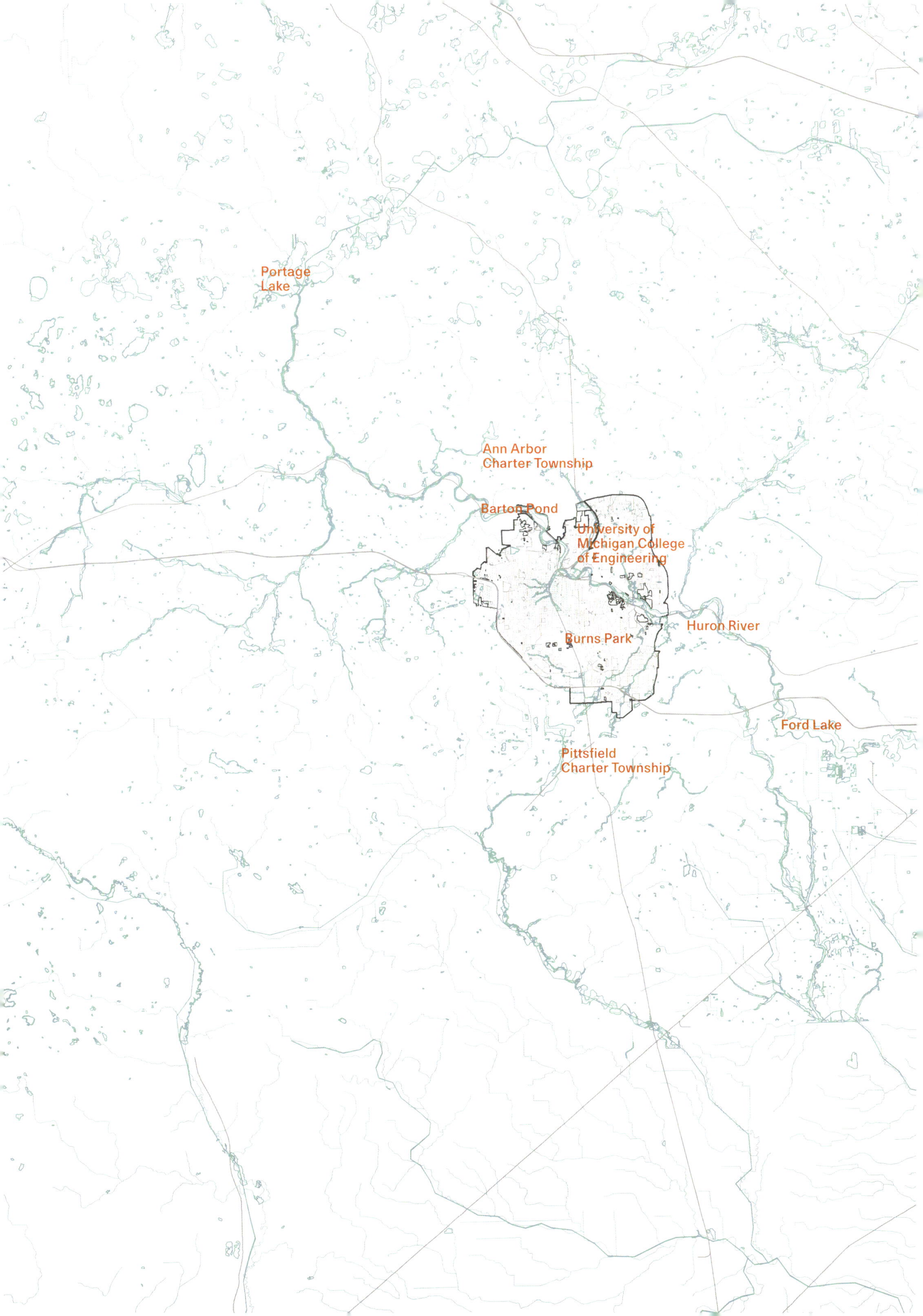
Portage Lake
Ann Arbor Charter Township
Barton Pond
University of Michigan College of Engineering
Huron River
Burns Park
Ford Lake
Pittsfield Charter Township

VOSTOK

CHALK
24

. . . water is everywhere before it is somewhere:
it is in rain before it is in rivers; it soaks,
saturates, and evaporates before it flows . . .

Anuradha Mathur and Dilip da Cunha

Bench Profile 1

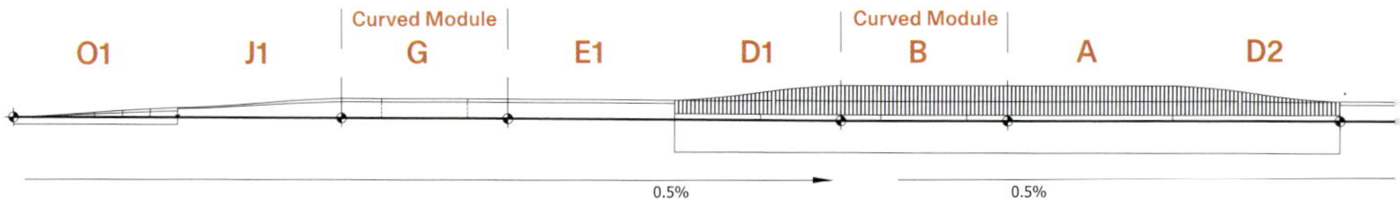

Bench Profile 2

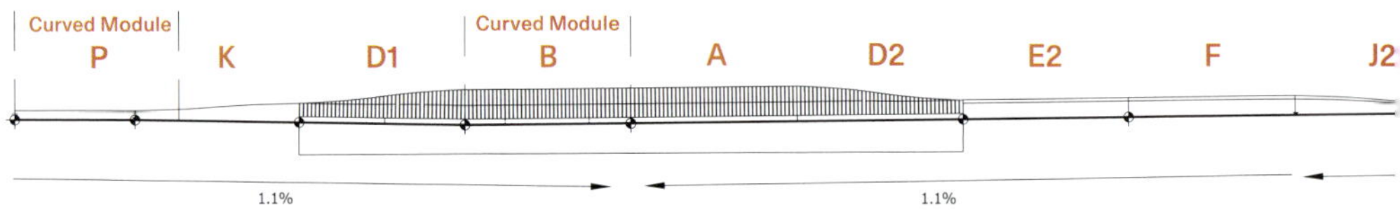

Bench Profile 3

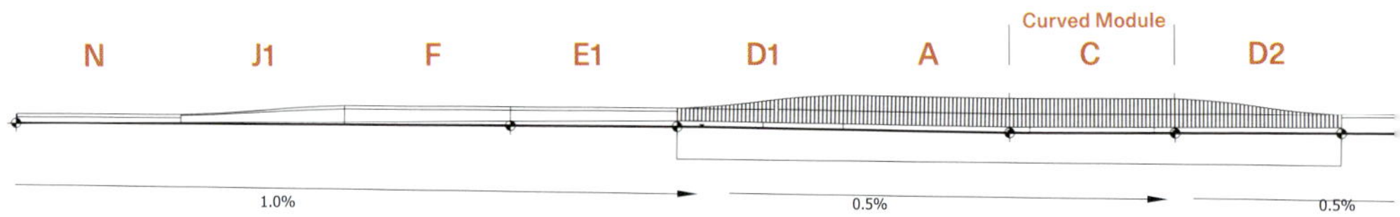

Bench Profile 4

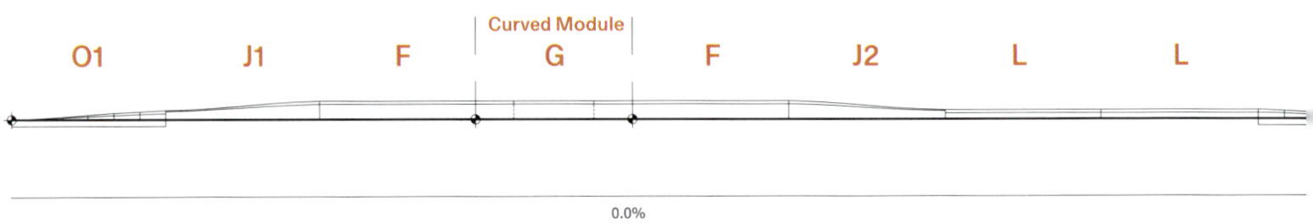

Bench Profile 5

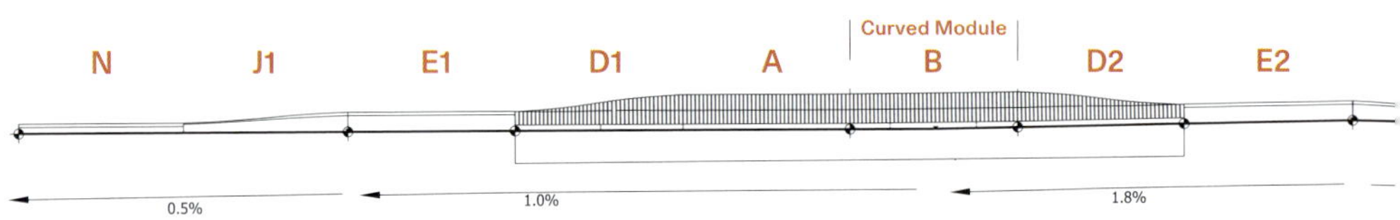

Bench Profile 6

Bench Profile 7

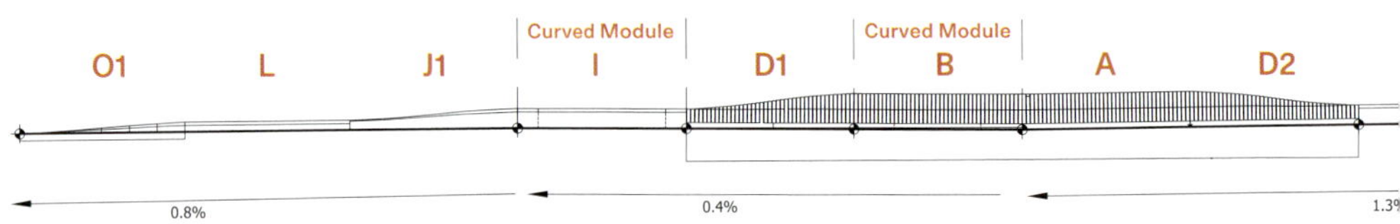

Sitting is hybridized with slope and drainage; bench-wall-curb configurations emerge from distinct, repeated modules combined and recombined and woven across 4 acres: 2243 linear feet in total.

Eda U. Gerstacker Grove, University of Michigan

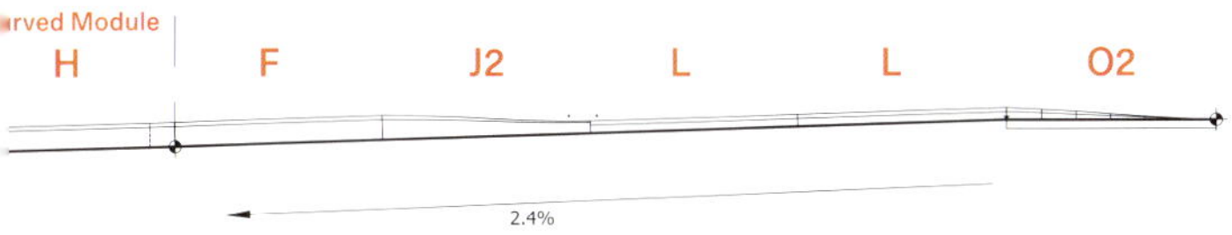
rved Module
H
F
J2
L
L
O2
2.4%

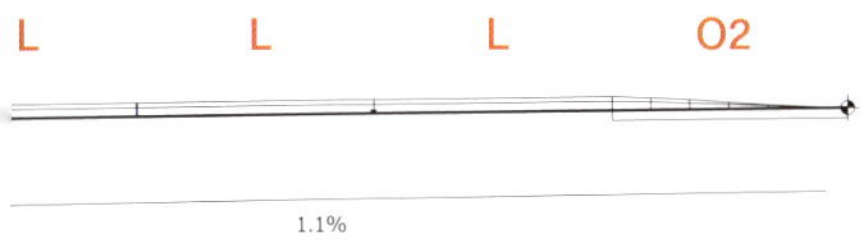
L
L
L
O2
1.1%

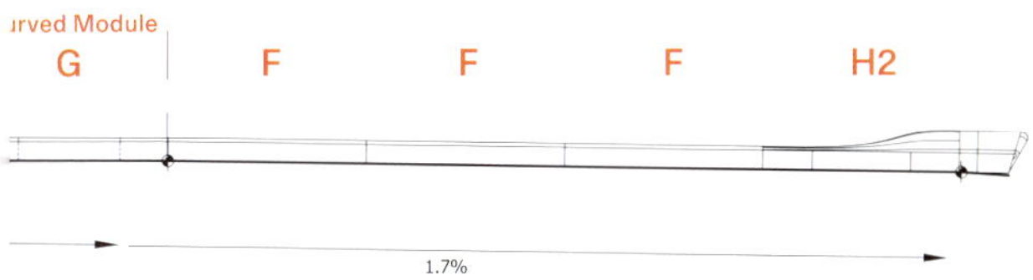
rved Module
G
F
F
F
H2
1.7%

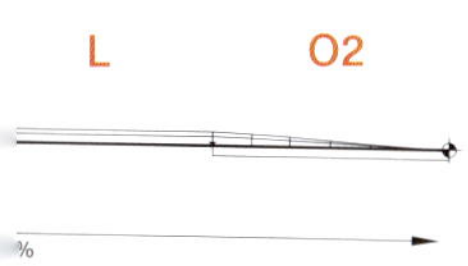
L
O2

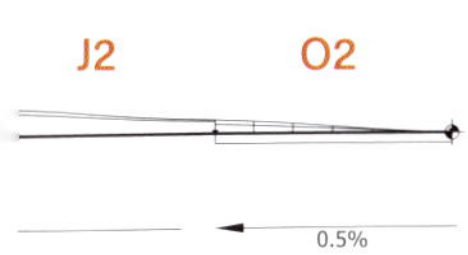
J2
O2
0.5%

120

A walk in town in spring, when everything is a mess, and different states of matter are in flux, is a walk through probability and chance. Euclid cannot help us here. The same logic governing continents, islands, and bays governs the puddle with its gravel, ice, sand, mud, and melting snow.

Teju Cole

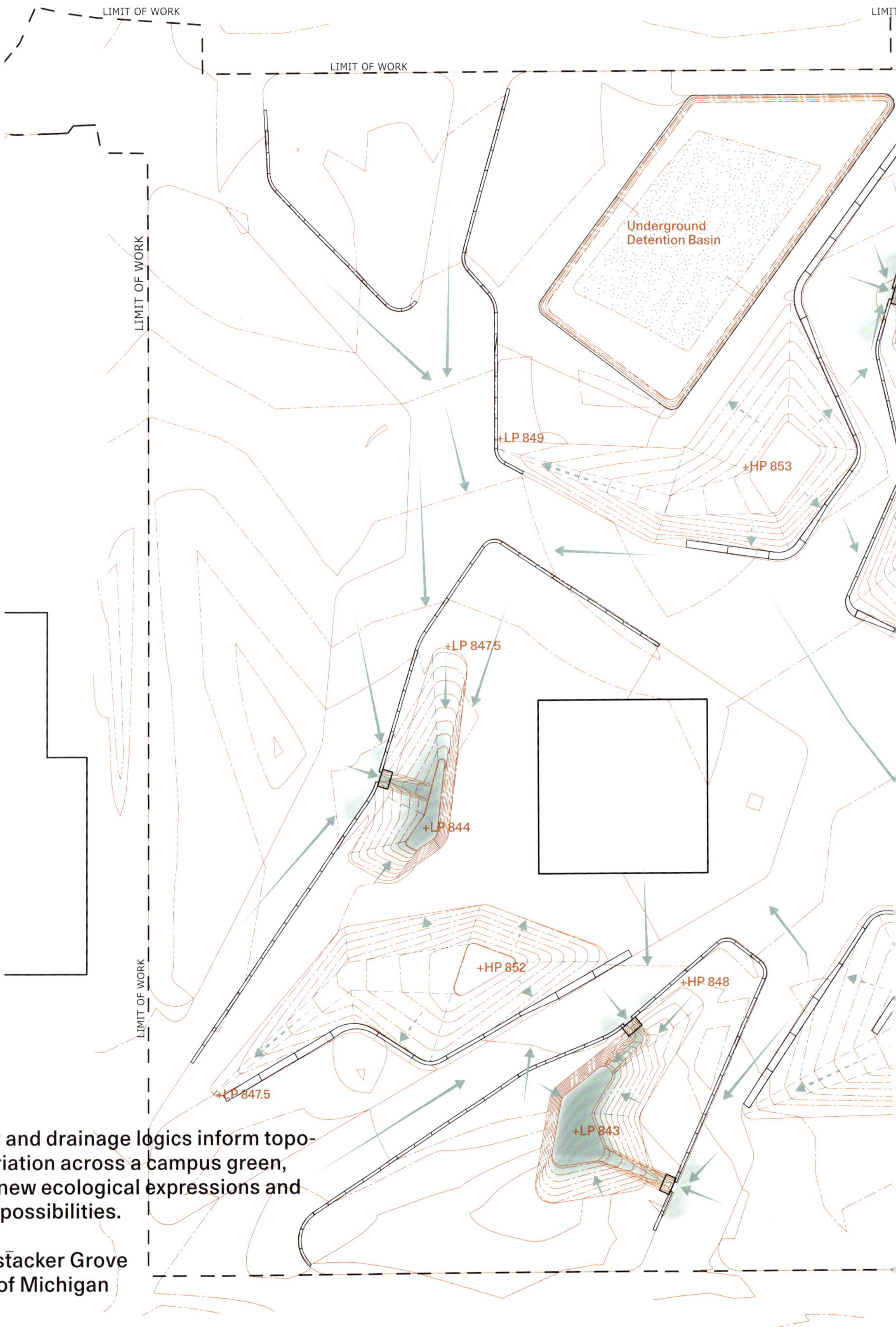

Circulatory and drainage logics inform topographic variation across a campus green, producing new ecological expressions and new social possibilities.

Eda U. Gerstacker Grove
University of Michigan

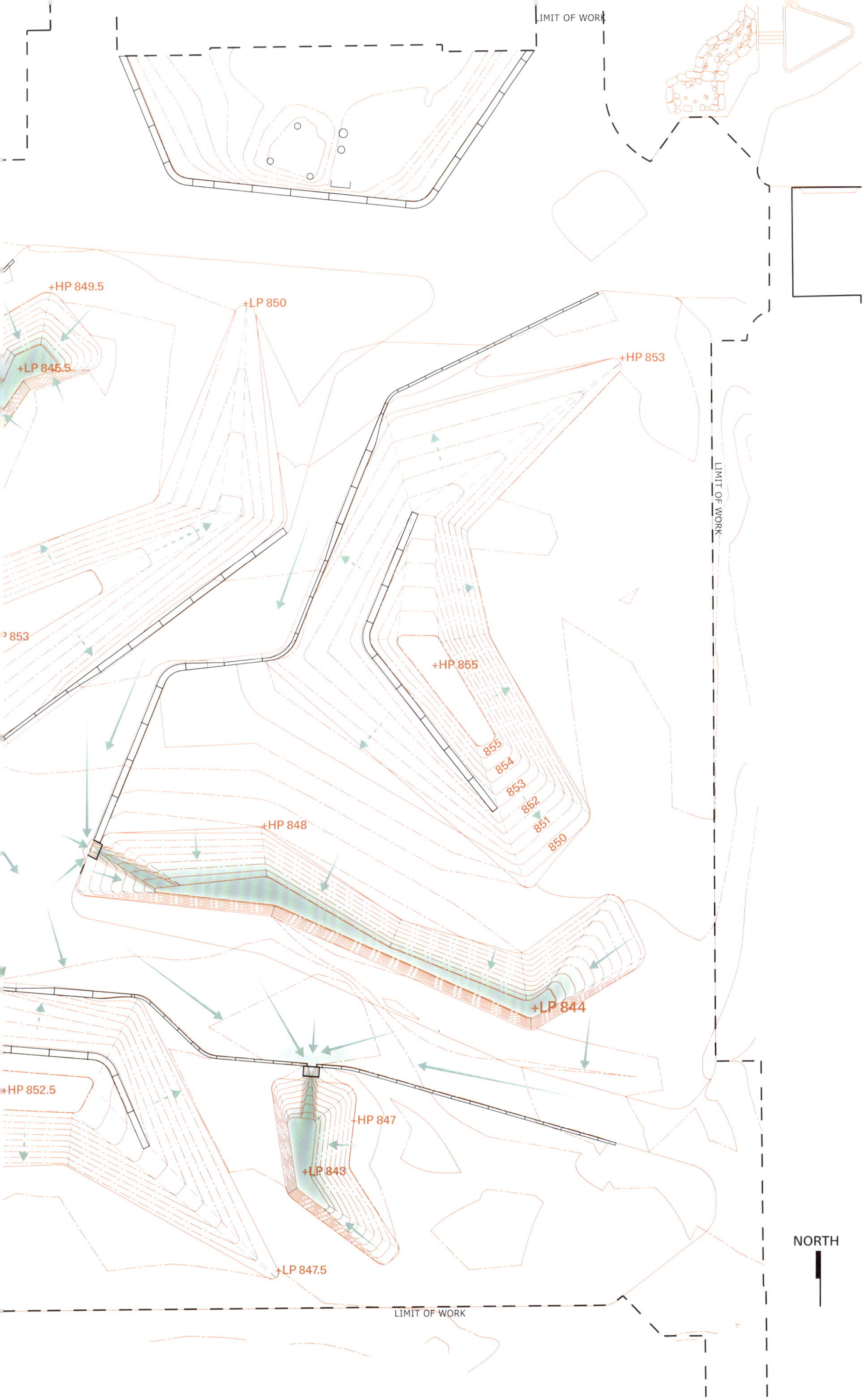

LIMIT OF WORK
+HP 849.5
+LP 850
+LP 845.5
+HP 853
LIMIT OF WORK
P 853
+HP 855
855
854
853
852
851
850
+HP 848
+LP 844
+HP 852.5
+HP 847
+LP 843
+LP 847.5
LIMIT OF WORK
NORTH

Appearance and (Aesthetic) Experience: The Ongoing Project of Stoss

Julia Czerniak

Prologue

2001
The Downsview Park Toronto international competition brings into sharp focus emerging design trends toward process-based urban landscapes, foregrounding disciplinary concerns around landscape's appearance and performance. My introduction to an edited volume examining this collective work explores the ways in which these design proposals expand our perception of how landscapes appear and perform—in other words, their process of becoming, the impressions they give, how they look, what they accomplish, and how they function. So preoccupied are the teams with their proposal's particular performativity (which privilege frameworks over form, engage complex processes like ecology, and favor dynamic change) that they say almost nothing about why their projects look the way they do. While I advance appearance and performance as provisional categories with which to frame discussions, I am especially interested in engaging questions such as: What is the effect of preoccupations with performance on appearance? Or, in simplified corollary terms, what is the relationship between how these park proposals "work" and how they "look"? Does a park conceived performatively inevitably and exclusively resemble these relations? Tree City—the winning entry by a team led by Rem Koolhaas and Bruce Mau—certainly suggests otherwise. Landscape's appearance, it becomes clear, can also be preoccupied with a parallel set of concerns. ("Appearance, Performance: Landscape at Downsview," 2001)[1]

2008
Elizabeth K. Meyer points to what the appearance/performance dialog to her mind has overlooked—namely, how appearance *performs*. Drawing on thinkers as diverse as Frederick Law Olmsted and Anne Whiston Spirn, she links appearance and performance through the discipline of aesthetics. She then inserts these concerns into the discourse of sustainability in the hopes of generating environmental engagement. In doing so she reminds landscape architects that discussions of beauty or aesthetics differ from discussions of the visual or the formal. Here, "aesthetics" includes how the experience of a designed landscape's forms and spaces (the things we make) work to alter our consciousness (through sensing, using, and thinking). ("Sustaining Beauty. The Performance of Appearance: A Manifesto in Three Parts," 2008).[2]

2010
Maria Hellström Reimer asserts, by drawing on landscape-related art practices, that landscape aesthetics reflective of our "agitated times" require a reconsideration of that which is consoling and beautiful toward an articulation of unsettled, intricate, and entangled spaces of transformation and change. She draws on French philosopher Jacques Rancière's seminal writing on the spatial "'distribution of the sensible'" to suggest that "aesthetics makes us aware of... the different modes of activating a certain set

of possibilities, be it the page, the stage, the canvas or—the landscape."[30–31] This potential activation of a vibrant and unstable publicity, she argues, makes us mindful of an important aesthetic dislocation, from representation and contemplation to agency. Aesthetics, Reiner asserts, "is not a sphere where you feel 'at ease'."[36] ("Unsettling eco-scapes: aesthetic performances for sustainable futures," 2010).[3]

2012
The editors of *Journal of Landscape Architecture* (JoLA)[4] bring aesthetics more comprehensively into discussions of ethics in their first themed issue. Including aesthetics forms what they call the "classic tripartite definition" of landscape architecture's disciplinarity: ethics, ecology, *and* aesthetics (in contrast to most conventional qualification of landscape's sustainability triad through the lens of equity, environment, and economy). They advance that "an aesthetics for today is one that is constituted through the acknowledgement of reality: the physical actuality, specificity and impermanence of every place"[5] rather than the envisioning of an idealized utopia. Aesthetic experience here emerges from the "physical and social actuality of landscape as lived,"[4] reinforcing a shift away from the simple contemplation Reimer previously described ("Editorial Ethics/ Aesthetics," *Journal of Landscape Architecture*, 2012).[5]

2015
Elizabeth Meyer revisits her widely cited 2008 essay, pondering the role sustainable aesthetics (not simply sustainable beauty) plays in sustainability agendas. She describes aesthetics as "an experience, not a formal language, not surface appearance,"[35] grounding her belief in geographer Nigel Thrift's assertion that aesthetics be understood as "a fundamental element of human life and not just an additional luxury."[35] Meyer notes that aesthetic experience requires duration and exists in the exchange between what ones sees/experiences and what one knows. She turns to theories of affect to unpack the agency of aesthetics in sustainability discourse. Theories of affect, she explains, entangle bodies, technologies, and networks across scale. A landscape architecture of affects, Meyer offers, is a social aesthetic that is provisional and speculative, where bodies adapt—and adapt to—each other and to space. By way of example, she relates her own aesthetic experience of an Australian garden, an affectual experience that "values the fluctuating, the particular, and the dense force field that weaves together encounter and memory, event and network, perception and cognition, experience and action."[41] ("Beyond 'Sustaining Beauty': Musings on a Manifesto," 2015).[6]

2016
Barbara Prezelj and Heidi Sohn bring affect theory to a discussion of landscape architecture and urbanism, which they reconceptualize as an "*action,*" rather than a "*thing.*" Reflecting on built work that landscape urbanism in particular has yielded, they suggest that—due in no small part to computer modeling and process-based design generation techniques—it verges on "carefully aestheticized representations" that fail to live up to the movement's promise of change and dynamic performance. The authors argue that although landscape urbanists reject "romantic, pastoral, or picturesque landscape scenes" in favor of dynamic relationships, they actually affirm them, and care deeply about the "aesthetic appeal of [their] projects' representations." Additionally, they argue that "ecological performativity is aesthetic" when aesthetics is understood as "affective, enabling potentials" rather than representational qualities. Here, "a body's behavior in relation to other bodies, in specific socio-material formations and provisional orderings"[30] reshapes our capacities to understand the world differently and

to change the way we think and act. This formulation extends the preoccupation with material, visible change evident in so much design work since the Downsview Park schemes (such as setting in motion the emergence of habitats, programming urban surfaces, etc.) to a more elusive set of lived experiences. The authors' call for landscape urbanism practices to embrace what the encounter with landscape *does* in this more refined and sophisticated way—how it "reshapes our capacities to act"—reinforces ongoing disciplinary arguments ("Towards an Aesthetics of Affect for Landscape Architecture/Urbanism," 2016).[7]

2018
Marc Treib stridently argues on behalf of landscape aesthetics—and by extension, appearance—outside of ethics. "Stressing performance or ethics alone," he warns, "abrogates the landscape architect's responsibility to... truly *design* aesthetically attractive landscapes."[30, 32] Quoting philosopher Roger Scruton, Treib suggests beauty is a quality that surpasses utility, a quality he refers to as "something else": "[W]e appreciate beautiful things... for what they are in themselves—or more plausibly, for how they *appear* in themselves."[32] As to the nature of this quality, Treib offers that a designed landscape's beauty shifts in place and time, and is "derive[d] from a skillful interweaving of form, space, proportion, light, and colour, paired with the embrace of seasonal change, growth, a knowledgeable selection of vegetation, and a host of other natural processes that will guide the evolution of the new landscape."[32] His critique of proposals for a sustainable aesthetic in landscape architecture aside,[8] his foregrounding of appearance raises an important point: How *do* we talk about how something looks ("Ethics≠Aesthetics," *JoLA*, 2018)?[9]

STOSS's work may be best known for its engagement with landscape performance. Equally as compelling, however, is the firm's preoccupation with how landscapes appear, from how they look as spatial and material formations to the ways in which they come into being—technically, technologically, and through the process of design. While this book foregrounds the social lives of cities and the dynamics that STOSS's designs activate, what follows here is a foray into the "project" of STOSS—an ongoing set of concerns and sensibilities that evolve over time. I emphasize "project," as opposed to "practice," intentionally, drawing loosely from a distinction articulated by architect Peter Eisenman. "If you have a project it is the [landscape] architect who defines the world around him or her," he explains. "If you have a practice, it is the world that defines you. Every project is always a critique of the status quo and of the discipline. So therefore, a project in some ways is always political, ideological, and intellectual."[10]

Four built works—two public waterfronts and two campus spaces—provide the materials with which I unpack STOSS's "project." How do the designers think about their work, outside of the services they provide and the needs of their clients? What design sensibility travels with them from site to site? How do accumulated knowledge, experimentation, reiteration, and construction impact its evolution? My hope is to articulate two distinct but not unrelated aspects of STOSS's work: first, its appearance, for the discussion of which I will draw from site visits, project descriptions, construction documents, and conversations with the designers. My distinction between appearance and performance here is provisional and is not intended to reinforce the binaries that have burdened our discipline for centuries (such as natural/artificial, formal/informal, science/art) nor do damage to the richness of the terms. I do so solely to address the dearth of discussions of appearance, in the field generally and in STOSS's work specifically. Second, I will speculate on

Figs. 1 and 2: Organizational logics of Erie Street Plaza

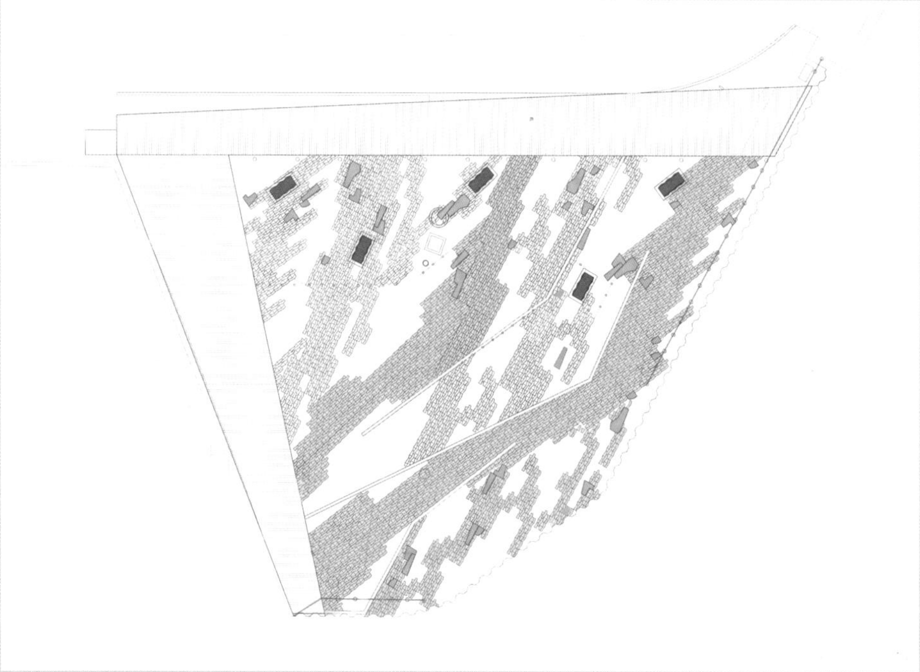

the aesthetic experience this work may be said to sponsor (as well as share my own experience) by using interpretations from the landscape thinkers cited above, supported by lived relations, historical documents, recent media coverage, and regional maps. Doing so allows us to probe some more general disciplinary questions, such as: How do more nuanced uses of the words "appearance"(a noun that implies apparent form or look) and "appear" (a verb that suggests the process of coming into being) help us view, understand and talk about landscapes? Does this framework enable us to elaborate on the role of appearance in aesthetic experience, which is

Fig. 3: A wetland marsh, concrete wall, plankstone pavers and plexiglass objects at the river's edge are some of the material systems and formal attributes of the site

connected to but not defined by it? And can we, from a field increasingly characterized by digital design practice, lend new insight to the appearance/performance conversation?

Waterfront Cities: Milwaukee and Green Bay, Wisconsin

STOSS completed its designs for two public waterfronts in Wisconsin within a span of two years. Erie Street Plaza, in Milwaukee (construction documents 2006; completed 2010), is a public landscape in the historic Third Ward of the city, at the confluence of the three rivers: the Milwaukee, the Kinnickinnic, and the Menomonee. This small, quarter-acre, triangularly shaped parcel is part of a string of public spaces along the Milwaukee Riverfront, a three-mile bike and pedestrian corridor that connects the downtown to the lakefront. For those familiar with STOSS's work, the intention here is a familiar one: to create as a flexible field that fosters social and environmental activity and appropriation. CityDeck, in Green Bay (construction documents 2008; completed 2013) is a quarter-mile linear park located along the Fox River in the city's downtown. Part of a more comprehensive mixed-use redevelopment project, its intention is to not only fill in vacant parcels but reconnect Green Bay residents with their waterfront, which has long been neglected and inaccessible. With ambitions not dissimilar to those of Erie Street Plaza, STOSS wanted through design and programming to create a flexible space for civic gatherings that would infuse downtown Green Bay with new life and reanimate the river's edge with a collective social presence.

Appearance, *noun*: the state or form in which a person or thing appears; apparent form, look, aspect; outward look or show, esp. as distinguished from reality[11]

I visited both of these works in late summer, long after construction was finished. Although natural processes and use have transformed their sites, their organizational systems, material logics, and spatial and formal attributes remain immediately legible. The design of Erie Street Plaza is a rich mosaic made up of diverse materials at different scales that gradually steps down to the historic river estuary on shallow terraces, separated by low retaining walls. Its paving, planting, and furnishing are disciplined by a diagonal pattern, loosely oriented by the geometry of street and river. This organization creates spaces for hardscape (weathered decking, exposed aggregate plankstone, and large concrete pavers) as well as softscape (groups of trees, expanses of grass, and a wetland marsh). A grove of poplar trees cluster at the site's edge and shield the street. Bands of grass in the plaza's center are vaguely defined by a paving that lacks a distinct edge, as if to suggest flexibility and work unfinished. Both give way to a lush wetland marsh, where perforations in a corrugated steel bulkhead enable river water to spill onto the plaza. Across the site, yellow plexiglass objects (which provide lighting at night) manifest the plaza's organizational patterns at the scale of the body. Arranged in various configurations and set at different heights, they provide individuals or groups with places to sit, stand, or lean. As objects without orientation, they also enable visitors to choose their own view toward the river, toward each other, toward the street. (figs. 1–3)

Figs. 4 and 5: Organizational logics of CityDeck

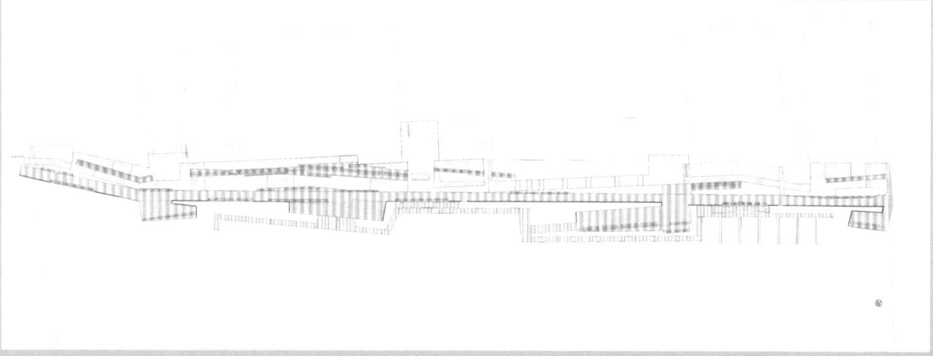

CityDeck's bands of silvery gray boardwalk and custom green pavers as well as expanses of lush lawn are organized to facilitate flow both to and along the Fox River. This formal and material logic is further articulated at pedestrian entrances, where the linear system thickens to become a stage, an amphitheater, an urban bench, and a dock for boaters. These breakout spaces have subtly different relationships to the river. One gradually slopes to its edge, another steps down by shallow risers to water level, and a third inclines from deck level to form a subtlety raised overlook. This sectional play extends to the treatment of upper terraces, which both rise and widen to accommodate programs such as restaurants and building entrances, offering users places to rest above the circulation along the deck. Although it is easy to mistake the design's smooth linearity as continuous, there is a hierarchy and site-specificness to its patterning, to which the project's abstract language is quite responsive. The decking, which folds to become furnishing, is complex and anthropomorphically scaled on the urban edge of the site, whereas broad and sweeping toward the river. Similarly, its density and intensity increase near entrances and around commercial development yet normalize as individual benches adjacent to residential uses. In these ways, the design's continuity of material systems

Fig. 6: The material palette consists largely of IPE wood decking, turf, and permeable and standard concrete pavers

together with its subtle variations in plan and section draw one to the river. (figs. 4–6)

Appear, *verb*: to come forth into view; to become visible[12]

Erie Street Plaza and CityDeck illustrate STOSS's emerging design sensibility and process. They organize both projects by patterning the site surface, which produces a language for two- and three-dimensional articulation and shaping.[13] This is most evident in the project's furnishings: analogically designed as separate modules and then arranged on site for variation, they produce a design interest the firm describes as "customized but mass produced."[14] At Erie Street Plaza, the shape of the fiberglass benches are simple extrusions of the site's surface pattern. Four bench types are built independently yet arranged as six groups, positioned to enable multiple variations in shape and use. CityDeck extends the firm's interest in patterning and variation toward facilitating greater movement and flow. Here their use of technology (although still AutoCAD) indexes their emerging preoccupation with replicability. The strings of urban furniture are made from six truss types that support eleven modules of different widths, heights, and configurations. Mass produced and fabricated off site, these frames are then clad in-situ by local carpenters. The firm's interest in inexpensive customization and the variation it enables is also evidenced in the exposed aggregate paving for CityDeck. Multiple, slightly varied elongated hexagonal shapes were made with one mold, and the pavers non-standard color was enabled by specifying previously used custom aggregate mixes. (figs. 7–8)

Beauty and Other Aesthetic Experience

If the appearance of a project (its process of becoming, its apparent look) is largely in the hands of the designer, its beauty and other aesthetic experiences are not. At Erie Street Plaza I was struck by many subtle aspects of its composition: the vertical repetition of the poplar grove's white trunks, slightly bent by the persistent wind; a branching structure just

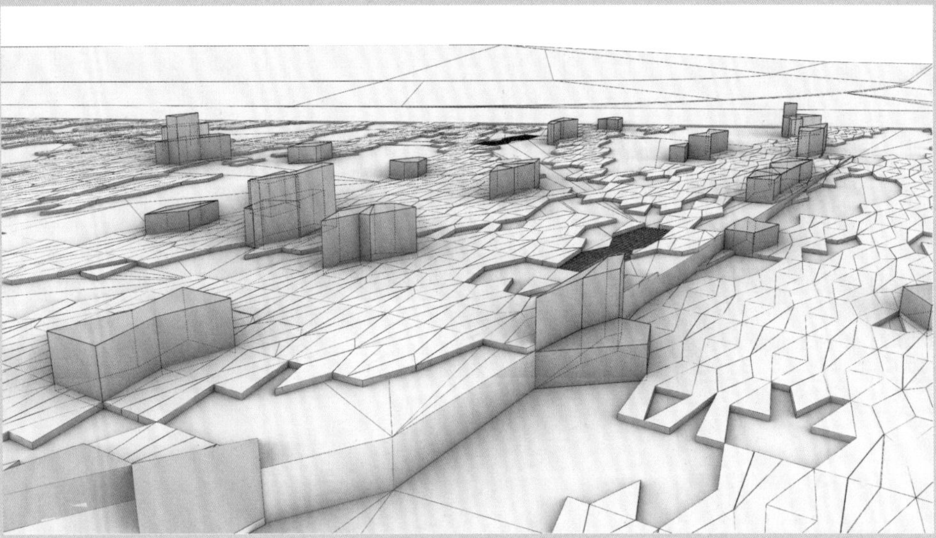

Fig. 7: Erie Street Plaza's site surface pattern and bench extrusions

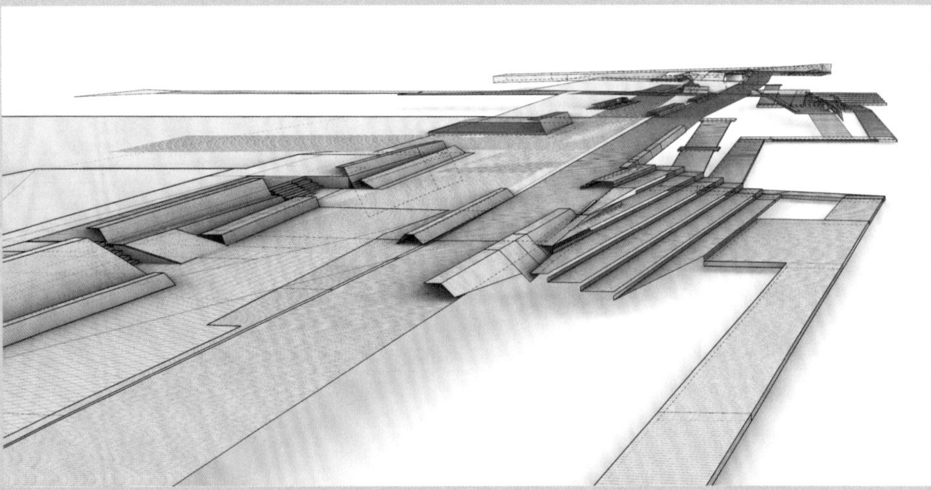

Fig. 8: CityDeck's replicable modules of urban furniture

high enough to frame views of the river; the rusty bulkhead wall's stark juxtaposition with the wetland plants, their lush greens inundated by a recent storm; the setting sun's brief, vibrant illumination of the yellow benches just before nightfall. (figs. 9–10) The diurnal cycles of light also transform CityDeck. Early morning rays slip through both deck entrances and boardwalk gaps, producing a contrasting shadow pattern across scale. By mid-day, the sharp afternoon sun accentuates the folds of the urban furniture. Tree shadows blur the edges between the wood, grass, and stone. At river level the graphic patterns of duckweed morph, as water laps the edge with each passing boat. Sunset washes both city and landscape in a pink glow. (figs. 11–12) If, as Treib suggests, beauty is a quality that "derives from a skillful interweaving of form, space, proportion, light, and color, paired with the embrace of seasonal change, growth, a knowledgeable selection of vegetation," then these landscapes surely are.

In addition to interpretating these works based largely on how they look and their design process, we can reflect on them as both individual and social aesthetic experiences, as Meyer, Reimer, Prezelj, and Sohn suggest. Most apt in this case is an interpretation that "weaves together encounter and memory, event and network, perception and cognition,

Fig. 9: Rusty bulkhead juxtaposed with lush wetland plants

Fig. 10: Illuminated furnishing at sunset

experience and action."[15] I visited Erie Street Plaza one lovely, late-August Saturday. Rowers were out early on the still water, while seagulls culled overhead. The site was damp and empty, and I was struck in this stillness by the juxtaposition of the site with the industrial nature of the landscape beyond. By lunchtime, the open field was activated by children playing games and families eating. Bike riders rested in the shade of the poplars. The river was alive with motorboats, bar barges, kayaks, and pedal boats. Yet I was drawn by the design itself not just to the water but to its *level,* and to the visceral experience it affords. (fig. 13) I recalled the history of Milwaukee as indigenous land, its name meaning at once "good earth," "good place," and "gathering place."[16] The word refers to the trading and meeting site where the three rivers that flow through Wisconsin join the lake. While standing adjacent to this fragment of reconstructed marsh I thought about how this estuary—long ago abundant in food sources and rich in wildlife—was a gift to the earliest of inhabitants, and my commitment to the restoration efforts of deindustrializing sites was renewed.

The streets of Green Bay were empty that day, but CityDeck was lively and crowded. The urban furniture was being used variously, as intended: groups gathered for picnics; people were sitting alone, reclining, even lying flat. This was especially evident adjacent to the exterior dining space of Hagemesiter Park, a restaurant whose name references the home of the Green Bay Packers in 1919. I was drawn to the amphitheater, far from the crowd and close to the river. While lying there, my eyes closed to the afternoon sun, the din of the crowd was cut only by the burr of motorboats passing by, followed by a quiet lap of water as it hit the bulkhead. I imagined this space across time—the river rife with ships at dock; the subsequent arrival of the railroad; the site's eventual use for parking, as development crowded its shore—and I felt thankful for all those who worked to return it to us, and us to it. By evening, the demographic had changed again. Groups of children played on the furnishings while teenagers gathered to skateboard; others, to play the guitar. A few loners with their dogs sat quietly. (fig. 14) The restaurant, with fire pits roaring, was even more crowded—filled with spectators, watching the sunset.

My experiences of these waterfront landscapes—as an "external

Fig. 11: Deck folds in the afternoon sun

observer"[17]—was influenced by my disciplinary knowledge, my encounter with these sites, conversations with the designers, and my understanding of the physical and cultural evolution of landscape. Yet it was encounters with others that recast this experience from a personal one to a social one. Through experiences of the "insider-participant"[18]—members of a community that have grown up in cities such as Milwaukee and Green Bay and experienced their transformations—I grew more deeply informed. Their rivers have familiar histories: they were a source of life and spirituality for early Native Americans; they were a means of transportation that facilitated trade for explorers, settlers, and colonists; and, much later, they were devastated environmentally through urbanization and industrialization. In the late twentieth century, city leaders invested in the rehabilitation of these rivers with the intent to stimulate economic growth.

Few know that Milwaukee's estuary was filled with wetlands and marshes, where Native Americans collected wheat. But Tony—the man fishing for trout and perch at Erie Street Plaza the day I was there—did. A barber by trade, Tony is an Italian American resident who grew up in the Third Ward, Milwaukee's oldest center of commerce and warehousing built

Fig. 12: Shadow patterns on duckweed and deck

Fig. 13: River and rain overflow register the water level on the site

after the land, regarded as a swamp, was drained and filled.[19] Erie Street Plaza is now a meaningful part of the neighborhood. Tony explained: "I've been coming here for years. I love it. It's sheer perfection." I noticed he was standing next to the constructed marsh, and I asked him why he chose that spot. "I like being as close as possible to the water. It is beautiful," he said, pointing to his catch, to the ducks, and to the bumblebees. "There is nothing better." (fig. 15) I also met a group of four women gathered on a Sunday afternoon at CityDeck to protest the Green Bay police's citizen arrest of Black Lives Matter protesters the night before.[20] By the time we spoke, the gathering had dissolved, but we chatted a bit about the site. Julie, Sophie, Morgan, and Jalynn described the importance of this river walk to them. They shared that it is at once a quiet place to clear their minds and a celebratory place for civic events, as well as a great backdrop for prom pictures and Instagram selfies. Most significantly, it is a place to feel connected to civic concerns regarding terrifying events as they currently unfold in our country.[21] (fig. 16)

I am reminded of the context for and lyrics of American poet and gospel music composer Robert Lowry's nineteenth-century hymn *Shall We Gather by the River*. It was 1864, a summer of oppressive heat, unease and despair as the Civil War divided the country. Many New Yorkers were suffering from fever, confining them to their beds.[22] Reverend Lowry's hymn is about "laying down our burdens and singing a melody of peace."[23] It was exuberant and hopeful, unfolding first as a question ("Shall we gather…?"), then as a proclamation ("Yes, let's gather…!"), and then as anticipation ("Soon we'll reach the shining river; Soon our pilgrimage will cease; Soon our happy hearts will quiver; With the melody of peace."). Tony, the Brown family, and I no doubt sense, use, and contemplate these waterfronts in vastly different ways. These experiences make us think differently as we join many who, for long periods of time, were drawn to the rivers for both commerce and sustenance, to gather there for recreation, protests, and peace. These designs facilitate our return. Here Reimer's landscape aesthetics—reflective of our "agitated times," where "landscape beauty turns performative and transformative"—is an apt interpretation.

Fig. 14: Children play on the deck furnishing at sunset

Campus Landscapes: Harvard Plaza and Gerstacker Grove

Two recent STOSS projects—campus spaces at Harvard University and the University of Michigan—illustrate the continuously emerging design sensibility of the firm. The Plaza at Harvard, in Cambridge, Massachusetts (construction documents 2012; completed 2013), is a deck that links the historic campus of Harvard Yard to the North Campus. It crosses over the four lanes of Cambridge Street and Broadway and acts as a "programmed urban surface" reminiscent of the ponderings of Alex Wall in his very influential essay.[24] The Eda U. Gerstacker Grove, in Ann Arbor, Michigan (construction documents 2015; completed 2016), is a renovation of an underutilized, 4-acre quadrangle at the center of the University of Michigan's North Campus. Both projects fully articulate a new campus space typology reflective of changes in higher education and in landscape's visibility. In addition, their appearances are strongly influenced by the emerging technologies that produce them.

Appearance, *noun*:

Harvard Plaza was busy when I visited in early October. Both the red Adirondack chairs and the custom wood benches were full of students working or eating, some from the resident food trucks parked on site. This activity masked a subtle but rich surface design. Predominantly concrete, the paving is organized by straight line segments that shift in direction to create bands of varying width, presumably corresponding to the deck structure below. The materials transition in relation to context, from brick on the historic Harvard Yard side to asphalt toward the Science Center and the Tanner Fountain, an important landscape feature. Embedded within this surface are a series of tie-downs that enable the installation of tents of multiple sizes, evidently used seasonally for a variety of activities such as farmers' markets, music performances, and ice-skating. The flexibility afforded by this hardware is expanded by the other moveable furnishings on site, such as umbrellas and planters that create flexible gathering spaces. The most visually striking element of the design is its smoothly contoured benches,

Fig. 15: Tony and his catch at the plaza's edge

Fig. 16: The Brown Family (Julie, Sophie, Morgan) and Jalynn Williams on deck after the Black Lives Matter march

which are placed to one side of the plaza and that float slightly above it. Although not extrusions of the plaza's organizational system precisely, they certainly relate to it as three-dimensional interpretations. The choice of unfinished Alaskan yellow cedar for their construction underscores the firm's interest in ongoing processes of formation. The surplus hardwood stock has weathered, split, and is now covered in lichen. The two edges of the plaza are lined with vegetation of radically different character. On the south side, deciduous hardwoods extend the canopy of trees in Harvard Yard over its wall, providing natural shade to those seated on the plaza below. On the north side, an unlikely pairing of ginkgos and staghorn sumac creates small spatial enclosures next to the Science Center. (fig. 17–20)

Gerstacker Grove is the largest of these four STOSS landscapes as well as their most recent. Here strategies of grading, planting, paving, programming, furnishing, and lighting combine to produce a spatially complex landscape space. Unlike the field logics of the prior work, the grove is organized by a large, irregular figure of varying intensities that provides circulation, creates spaces, and connects to a larger campus network. The edge of this figure is shaped by both serpentine and straight lines, articulated alternately by curb, bench, and wall, that frame the path. The lofted logic of the furnishing at Harvard Plaza is here extended into a seamless composition in plan and section. The shaped ground forms rise into gentle hills and fall to create infiltration gardens. The hills are enhanced by finely textured bosques and reinforced by no-mow grass, and the gardens are hyper-planted with shade-loving and water-tolerant herbaceous plants and trees intended to collect water. Planting here does not reinforce the hill geometry but counters it, contributing to a spatially ambiguous—almost disorienting—landscape in which to lose oneself. (fig. 21–24)

Appear, *verb*:

By the time STOSS designed Harvard Plaza and Gerstacker Grove early in the second decade of the twenty-first century, digital design practices were starting to gain traction in landscape architecture practice. The ongoing coincidence of interests in landscape performance, the agency of ecological thinking, and emerging technologies that enable ways to envision and generate landscapes is well documented.[25] Significant for landscape practice, this moment is characterized by landscape architect Jillian Wallis as "reflective of a different relationship

Figs. 17 and 18: Organizational logics, material palettes and site furnishing at Harvard Plaza

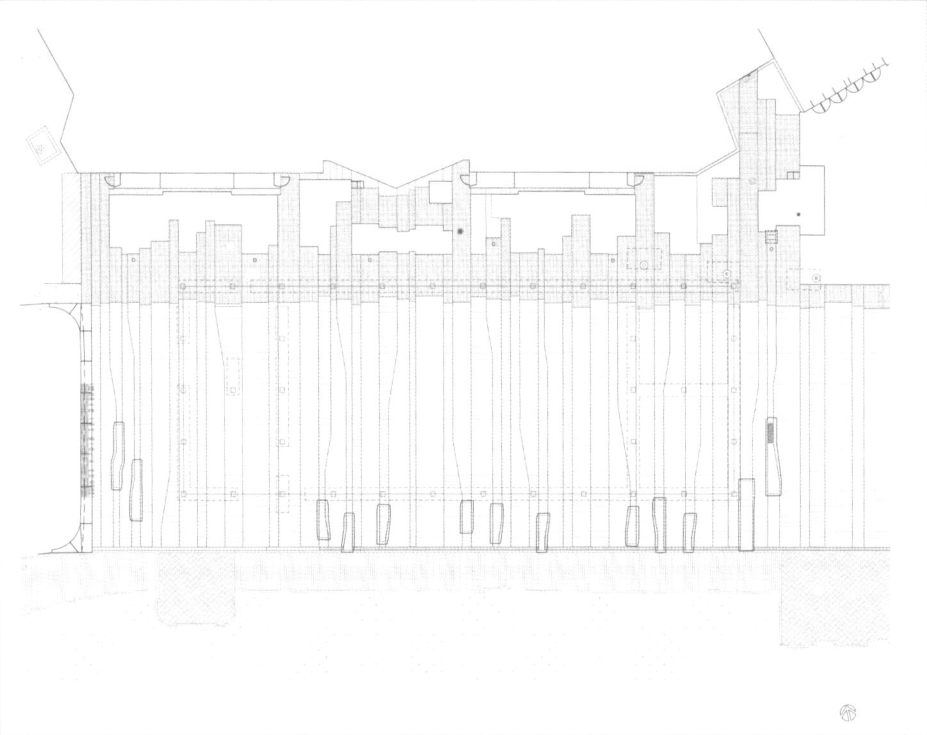

Fig. 19: Alaskan yellow cedar benches are smoothly contoured in relation to the body

Fig. 20: Deciduous hardwoods extend the canopy of trees over Harvard Yard's wall, offering shade for plaza users

between designer, information, and processes. Digital technologies move from the privileging of the visual and compositional to a focus on processes of formation."[26]

Although STOSS is not considered a digital design practice per se,[27] their use of emerging technologies to reconceptualize the design and fabrication of their work through parametric modeling and, most recently, responsive technologies, is strongly evident in its appearance. At both Harvard and Michigan, STOSS use digital models for both the intuitive, real-time explorations of form as well as for a rule-based approach to making, including the testing of parameters such as those for bodily comfort. For example, the design for Harvard Plaza's linear furnishings began in the office with a series of initial anthropomorphic inputs of the body in different positions as well as through generic and normalized data. The lofting between these distinct and measured profiles and control points created the smooth form where no "standard" rib is similar to the one next to it, yielding instead infinite variation based on the inputs. As a result, by slipping along the bench just a few inches one will experience a slightly different surface profile. This design process suggests that the relationship of—in this case an object's—appearance and performance are increasingly blurred. Additionally, the team intuitively (and unapologetically) adjusts the model based on their preferred design sensibility as a way of reconciling the quantitative benchmarks of performance with qualitative social factors such as preferences, desires, needs, and comfort. The digital model also affords a file-to-fabrication ease for building and maintenance. The 5-axis CNC router that machines complex shapes with efficiency and accuracy forms each rib as its own frame. Damaged components are easily replaced by a built-in tracking system. (fig. 25)

Whereas Harvard Plaza is essentially a flat plane treated as a field condition, the size and complexity of Gerstacker Grove enabled the designers to extend similar concerns to a larger and more varied site. Paving, curb, bench, wall, and topography are all disciplined by the parametric

Figs. 21 and 22: The spatially complex landscape of Gerstacker Grove is organized by a figure that connects to a larger campus network

Fig. 23: Curved, serpentine and straight lines—articulated by curb, bench and wall—frame the path

Fig. 24: Richly diverse infiltration gardens give way to gentle hills

model through inputs relating to slope and activity, soil and retention, bodies in motion and at rest. In keeping with their interest in customization, the designers used digital modeling (as compared to the analog techniques of earlier work) to achieve greater variation from a simple set of parts (fig 26). Additionally, the design's extensive use of plants reveals STOSS founder and design director Chris Reed's approach to the landscape medium. His planting strategy is strongly influenced by his early studies at the University of Pennsylvania, where field ecology and ecosystem dynamics were favored over ornamental or horticultural values. Given that most of the sites on which STOSS works are damaged or disturbed (by people, by salt, by other types of contaminates), it is virtually impossible to constitute a planting palette from regional choices. Their approach at Gerstacker Grove was driven more by questions such as: What ecology is suitable here? How might these plants adapt to a place in time? Northern hardwoods (oaks, maples, hickories) around the quad's perimeter form a dark threshold through which one passes into a light interior, planted with delicate amelanchier. The asymmetrical infiltration gardens, filled with ferns, hostas, and lillyturf and accented with bald cypress trees, are large and deep in order to store stormwater. The addition of acrylic rods with vibrant LEDs to these gardens not only reflects the firms growing experimentation with responsive technologies but also potentially amplifies the environmental changes that are so fundamental to their work: as stormwater enters the garden, the rods flicker, indexing the weather and heightening one's sensory experience.

Aesthetic (and Other) Experience

If aesthetic experience exists, as the voices in the beginning of this chapter suggest, in the exchange between what one sees and experiences and what one knows, my visits to Harvard Plaza and Gerstacker Grove were rich and engaged. I was not only taken by these projects' appearance(s), but also motivated to recall disciplinary concerns, such as the premises of landscape urbanism, emergent campus typologies, and theories of line and shape.

I visited Harvard Plaza on a cloudy late September day. Between the robust use of its amenities and the din of the streets below, I hardly recognized the design. The plaza read more as a setting leading me to recall geographer J.B. Jackson's formulation of landscape as "a composition of…spaces to serve as infrastructure

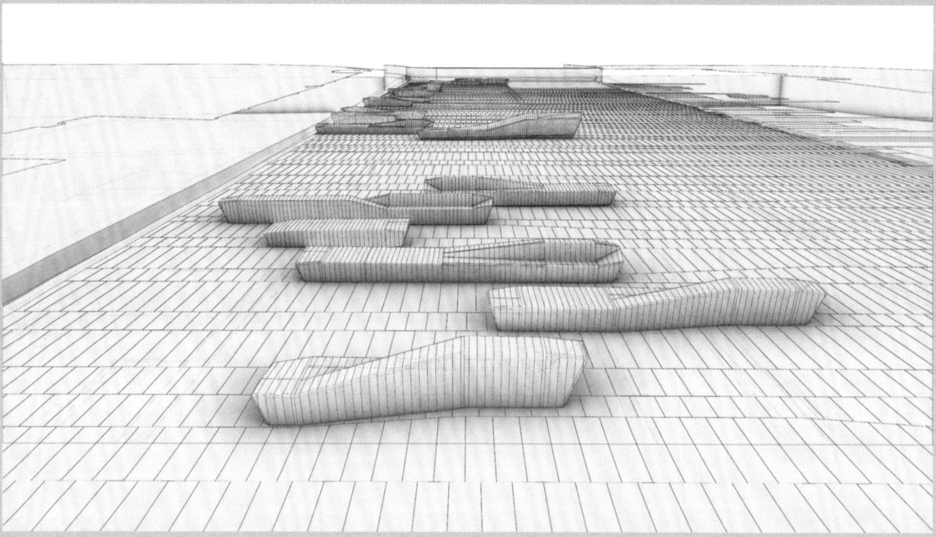

Fig. 25: The parametric model at Harvard Plaza is a reconciliation of quantitative benchmarks and qualitative factors

Fig. 26: Paving, curb, bench, wall and topography at Gerstacker Grove are all disciplined by the parametric model

or background for our collective existence."[28] In this way it is a fine example of a programmed urban surface—the landscape urbanist's ambition—and its successful completion and use almost twenty years after the movement's launch made me feel happy for the discipline. I was most struck by the plaza's juxtaposition to Harvard Yard, one of the oldest public spaces in the country. Whereas the plaza was boisterous, the yard, with its mature hardwoods set in a lush lawn, enclosed by Georgian buildings, seemed traditional, quiet, and cloistered, despite the pathways that crisscross it. (fig 27) In this way my experience of the present recalled the past, here an entire lineage of campus spaces where landscape (as topography, program, and surface) plays a primary role in their transformation: from Hargreaves Associate's figured and patterned grounds at the University of Cincinnati (1998), to Michael van Valkenburg's varied valley meadows and native plant communities at Wellesley College's Alumnae Valley (2005), to Field Operation's richly programmed campus perimeter of social spaces, intended to foster interaction and collaboration, at the Cornell Tech Campus (2017). On the one hand, these campus spaces certainly embed visions of community and challenge how traditional campus space looks and works. On the other, the lack of discernment in providing open, green, and actual (democratic) public space within revenue-driven institutions of higher education—which strive to make their campus's amenities "attractive" to their

Fig. 27: The traditional campus landscape of Harvard Yard

Fig. 28: Layers of lines move up the slope

Fig. 29: A curved line swells to create places to sit

consumers (tuition-paying students) and compete in the marketplace—is a territory that needs exploration.[29]

Gerstacker Grove fits within this lineage of new typologies of campus space, but when I visited it on a cold October morning, I became preoccupied by an entirely different set of concerns. Unlike the time I spent at a crowded Harvard Plaza, I had this space to myself in the morning light. I was transfixed by the lines, forms, and shapes that defined this landscape as I moved through it. At its most appealing were a play of lines made by the smooth, white concrete walls, and metal benches (reinforced by the scores in the pavement) against the manicured lawn, retaining walls, long grasses, and tree massings, as these elements moved up the slope. Even more striking was the way the lines swelled out to form sitting spaces and in again to encourage the movement of one's body through space. (figs. 28, 29)

Serpentine lines play an important role in landscape history. In *The Analysis of Beauty* (1753), William Hogarth famously suggests that such a line is unique in that it "leads the eye in a pleasing manner along the continuity of its variety": Hogarth terms it the "line of beauty."[30] More recently, the curators of an exhibition at the Princeton University Art Museum called *The Line of Beauty: Refiguring the Serpentine Line from Drawing into Photography* seek to trace the "intimacy, tactility, and allusive

Fig. 30: An animated serpentine line

Fig. 31: From above, spaces appear as carved shapes

capacity of this particular 'lively' line: a line that 'weaves' and 'winds' from the Quattrocento through the contemporary moment."[31] It was fascinating to recognize that the serpentine line at Gerstacker Grove was most powerful when it was singular, played against a straight line somewhere on the site. (fig. 30) The simplicity of this precise yet varied line appears in the provocatively curated Princeton exhibition within bodies, scribbles, geometric abstractions, ocean waves, and even hair.[32] I finished my visit by moving off the pathway, to traverse the grove in ways not necessarily suggested

Fig. 32

by the circulation system. From the top of one mound I had a better view of the shapes produced through the designers' manipulation of lines, and they looked more like carvings from a thick two-dimensional surface, an imprint within the ground that resonates with design theorist Robert Somol's advancement of arbitrary, cool shapes that offer graphic immediacy.[33] (figs 31, 32) As these observations suggest, my mental meandering through these materials were as complex as my spatial ones through this landscape, and the distinction between discussing the appearance of a work—in contrast to its aesthetic experience—became clearer.

—

If STOSS's "project" is in some way a critique of the status quo within landscape architecture—as Eisenman suggests such endeavors are—then this work as discussed pushes against the persistent position that the formal, spatial and material concerns of our discipline are inconsequential (or at least secondary) to the more responsible design efforts directed at achieving sustainable landscapes. As I began by saying, STOSS's work is known for—and largely discussed through—the way it performs. Indeed, these four projects perform a consequential amount of work: environmentally (from reusing waste materials [such as porcelain used as aggregate in pavers], to collecting and cleaning run-off and managing stormwater, to enabling biodiversity and sequestering carbon in newly planted trees and other vegetation); economically (for the cities and campuses where the projects reside); and socially (for the citizens that visit, use, occupy and love these projects). However, as I hope to have shown, this work *also* clearly and unapologetically advances a design agenda regarding landscape's appearance, in all of its complexity. In this way STOSS has developed a provocative both/and design sensibility: they *both* respond to the field's highest ethical responsibilities and external concerns *and* engage in their own internal preoccupation with the look of things as well as the technologies and processes used to make them.

And why might this matter? As the considerable thinking conducted over the last twenty years makes clear, appearance and aesthetic experience are not the same thing, although their meanings are entangled. Thinkers like Meyer have argued for the importance of both—even in the context of global health and planetary crises—in the pursuit and realization of sustainable environments. For many, this may be reason enough to foreground appearance, and STOSS's "project" shows us one way. But moving beyond this, I might suggest that it is precisely the attention given to a project's appearance, together with our ability to differentiate well-designed landscapes from ordinary everyday ones, that gives designed landscapes their agency to change the way we think about—and act within—our environment.

—

And yet, we must value appearance "in its own right," not just "in service of" other ambitions. After all, is it not our preoccupation with the visual, the spatial, the formal, and the material that defines us as designers and thus motivates all that we do?

Notes

All photos in this article by Julia Czerniak.

1 Julia Czerniak, "Appearance and Performance," in *CASE: Downsview Park Toronto*, ed. Julia Czerniak (Cambridge, MA: Harvard University Graduate School of Design, and New York: Prestel, 2001),10–19.

2 Elizabeth K Meyer, "Sustaining Beauty: The Performance of Appearance. A Manifesto in Three Parts," in *Journal of Landscape Architecture,* Volume 3-Issue 1 (Abingdon, Oxfordshire: Routledge, Taylor and Francis Group, 2008), 16–23.

3 Maria Hellström Reimer, "Unsettling Eco-scapes: Aesthetic Performances for Sustainable Futures," in *Journal of Landscape Architecture,* Volume 5 – Issue 1 (Abingdon, Oxfordshire: Routledge, Taylor and Francis Group, 2010), 24–37.

4 The *JOLA* editors at the time of this issue's publication were Bernadette Blanchon-Caillot, Catherine Dee, Anna Jorgensen, Karsten Jorgensen, Bianca Maria Rinaldi, and Kelly Shannon.

5 Caillot Blanchon, Catherine Dee Bernadette, Anna Jørgensen, Karsten Jørgensen, Bianca Maria Rinaldi, and Kelly Shannon, "Ethics/Aesthetics," in *Journal of Landscape Architecture,* Volume 3 (Abingdon, Oxfordshire: Routledge, Taylor and Francis Group, 2012), 4–5.

6 Elizabeth K Meyer, "Beyond 'Sustaining Beauty': Musings on a Manifesto," in *Values in Landscape Architecture & Environmental Design*, ed. M. Elen Deming (Baton Rouge: Louisiana State University Press, 2015): 30–54. It is interesting to note that cultural geographer Denis Cosgrove discusses the "affective aspect" of landscape in his chapter "The Idea of Landscape," in *Social Formation and Symbolic Landscape* (Madison: University of Wisconsin Press, 1984), 13–38, long before the turn to affect became instrumental to cultural criticism and cultural theory in the early to mid-1990s.

7 Barbara Prezelj and Heidi Sohn, "Towards an Aesthetics of Affect for Landscape Architecture/ Urbanism," in Proceedings, *Beyond ism: The Landscape of Landscape Urbanism* (Alnarp, Sweden: October 2016), 19–21.

8 Marc Trieb suggests "To date, continued arguments and proposals for a sustainable aesthetic by a select group of academics and professionals have been unconvincing and have consequently languished," and states that he "…must leave the final word (about beauty) to philosophers and art historians…" See Marc Treib, "Ethics≠Aesthetics" in *Journal of Landscape Architecture,* Volume 13 – Issue 2 (Abingdon, Oxfordshire: Routledge, Taylor and Francis Group, 2018) 30 and 33 for more context for these statements.

9 Treib, "Ethics≠Aesthetics," 30–41.

10 Peter Eisenman, "Practice or Project," lecture, delivered at Syracuse University School of Architecture, Sept 30, 2011]. https://www.youtube.com/watch?v=TnyJRYyuhHU&t=2268s&ab_channel=SyracuseArchitecture%28SyracuseUniversitySchoolofArchitecture%29

11 "appearance, n.". OED Online. September 2020. Oxford University Press. https://www-oed-com.libezproxy2.syr.edu/viewEntry/9555?redirectedFrom=appearance& (accessed December 01, 2020).

12 "appear, v.". OED Online. September 2020. Oxford University Press. https://www-oed-com.libezproxy2.syr.edu/view/Entry/9553? (accessed December 01, 2020).

13 I use the word "patterning" here in the way James Corner suggests: "Patterns are relational frameworks that simultaneously describe and project; they *reveal* structures, processes and relationships as well as *structure*

physical frameworks that give shape and form to our world." See his Foreword to Karen M'Closkey and Keith VanDerSys's, *Dynamic Patterns* (London: Routledge, 2017), vii–viii.

14 Chris Reed, "Generative Modeling and the Making of Landscape," in *Codify: Parametric Computational Design in Landscape Architecture,* ed. Bradley Cantrell and Adam Mekies (London & New York: Routledge Taylor & Francis Group, 2018), 50–63.

15 Meyer, ibid., 41.

16 Bonnie Petrie, "Mino-akking, Mahn-a-waukke: What's the Origin of the Word 'Milwaukee'?" NPR broadcast, October 14, 2016. https://www.wuwm.com/post/mino-akking-mahn-waukke-whats-origin-word-milwaukee#stream/0

17 Cultural Geographer Denis E. Cosgrove explains these two very different ways of understanding the world, and cites the difference between the "external, individual observer" and the "insider-participant." He suggests "the affective bond between human beings and the external world is not merely, perhaps not even primarily, an individual or personal thing. For geography, in fact the personal relationship is of minor importance when compared with the collective investment of meaning in places by those who make and keep them." See "The Idea of Landscape," in *Social Formation and Symbolic Landscape* (Madison: University of Wisconsin Press, 1984),13–38.

18 Ibid., 19.

19 Thanks to Tony Pullara for sharing his story with me on the site that day.

20 https://www.greenbaypressgazette.com/story/news/2020/08/30/jacob-blake-protests-rally-planned-sunday-afternoon-green-bay/3434823001/

21 I refer here to the recent murders of George Floyd (May 25, 2020); Breonna Taylor (March 13, 2020), and Ahmaud Arbery (February 23, 2020)—just a few of the victims of injustice in the United States.

22 This brilliant article, written in 2015, not only recounts the initial context in which Reverend Lowry wrote this hymn, but shows how history is repeating itself. It is 2020, and not much has changed. http://askherabouthymn.com/what-comforting-old-hymn-was-written-during-a-summer-of-misery-in-brooklyn/

23 Ibid.

24 Alex Wall, "Programming the Urban Surface," in *Recovering Landscape: Essays in Contemporary Landscape Architecture* (New York: Princeton Architectural Press, 1999), 233–250.

25 See the introductions of these important publications:
Jillian Walliss and Heike Rahmann, *Landscape Architecture and Digital Technologies* (London: Routledge, 2016).
Bradley Cantrell and Justine Holzman, *Responsive Landscapes* (London: Routledge, 2016).
Karen M'Closkey and Keith VanDerSys, *Dynamic Patterns* (London: Routledge, 2017).
Bradley Cantrell and Adam Mekies, eds., *Codify* (London: Routledge, 2018).

26 Wallis, Ibid., 206.

27 Although STOSS uses the tools of digital practice generatively, academic practices—such as PEG, Office of Outdoor Research/LMLab, and (gritlab)—that test the capability of these tools are more apt examples of DDP.

28 The full citation reads: "In the contemporary world it is by recognizing this similarity of purpose that we will eventually formulate a new definition of landscape: a composition of manmade or man-modified spaces to serve as infrastructure or background for our collective existence; and if background seems inappropriately modest we should remember that in our modern use of the word it means that which underscores not only our identity and presence, but also our history." The similarity

of purpose to which he refers is the profession of landscape architecture and civil engineering. See J. B. Jackson, "The Word Itself," *Discovering the Vernacular Landscape* (New Haven: Yale University Press, 1984), 1–8.

29 I draw here on work by cultural geographer Don Mitchell who suggests two contradictory ideals that drive the production of public space. The first understands public space as a space in which diverse publics meet, gather, and interact—not always amicably. It is a space of struggle, even if it is also a space of leisure, of recreation, and of consumption. The second ideal Mitchell outlines understands public space to be a controlled, orderly, well programmed space to which the public is invited—as long as it behaves itself. See "Downsview Park: Open Space or Public Space?" in *CASE: Downsview Park Toronto*, 102–115.

30 William Hogarth, *The Analysis of Beauty*, kindle edition (@AnnieRoseBooks: 2016)

31 This exhibition was curated by Anna Moser, Kate Thorpe, Denise Koller, and Regina Teng- as part of *HUM 598: Drawing and the Line in Lite*. See https://artmuseum.princeton.edu/object-package/line-beauty-refiguring-serpen tine-line-drawing-photography/43017.

32 Ibid.

33 Robert Somol, "12 Reasons to get back in Shape" in *Content*, ed., Rem Koolhaas (Cologne: Taschen, 2004), 86–87.

Detroit, Michigan

Detroit is a city on the rebound, a place where culture has long been built around food, music, art, and social life. People here are rediscovering and remaking their communities in the vibrant social scenes around Eastern Market with ad hoc vendors and street musicians; in the clubs where lifelong African American residents kick back, sometimes with an expanding audience of newcomers (often white, moving into the city after decades of white flight); and in neighborhoods where vacant lots are being made newly productive—all to re-invent the city and create a new and distinct form of shared urban living.

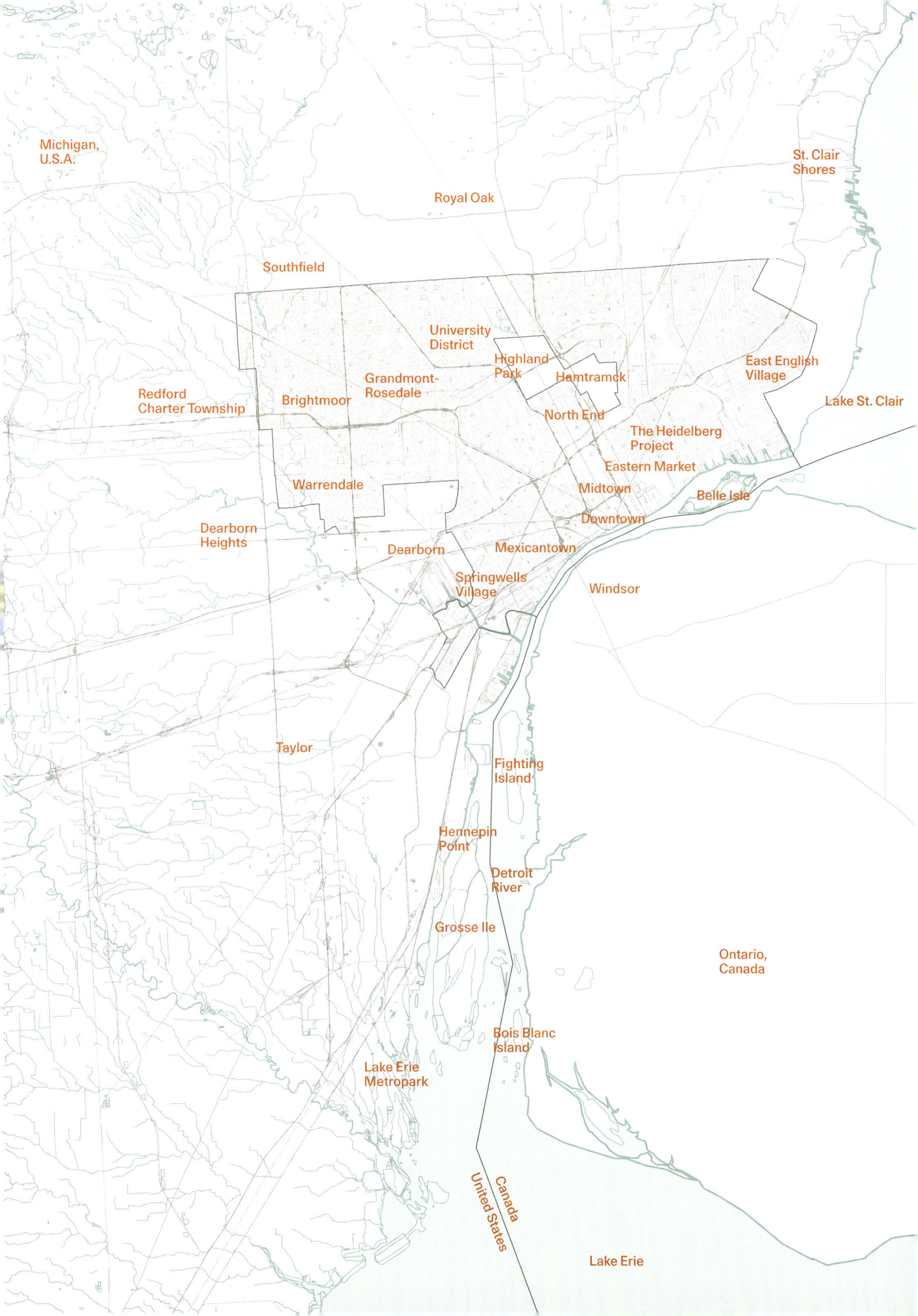
Michigan, U.S.A.
St. Clair Shores
Royal Oak
Southfield
University District
Highland Park
Hamtramck
East English Village
Grandmont-Rosedale
Redford Charter Township
Brightmoor
North End
Lake St. Clair
The Heidelberg Project
Eastern Market
Warrendale
Midtown
Belle Isle
Downtown
Dearborn Heights
Dearborn
Mexicantown
Springwells Village
Windsor
Taylor
Fighting Island
Hennepin Point
Detroit River
Grosse Ile
Ontario, Canada
Bois Blanc Island
Lake Erie Metropark
Canada
United States
Lake Erie

Magee's

PEPSI
PEPSI
PEERCORPS

We build, we correct what we have built, we break down what we have built, we build again, and correct again. Deconstruction is no more real than continuous construction. Things accrue. Renovation is the city's fact. It is the universal language, the second of the two seasons.

Teju Cole

GR ce

faith
FAITH

UNITY · DREAM · FAITH · HOPE · DANCE · LAUGH
PEACE · JOY · LOVE · HAPPINESS

Love
15847

HOPE

PEACE

ROOF

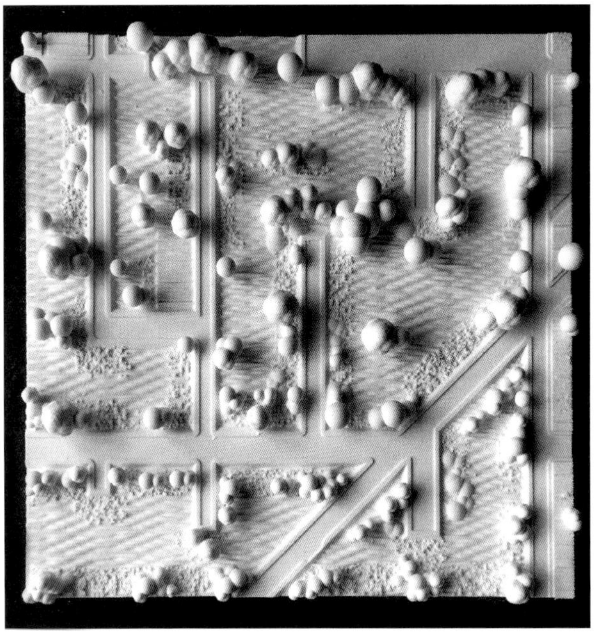

01. Blue + Green Infrastructure

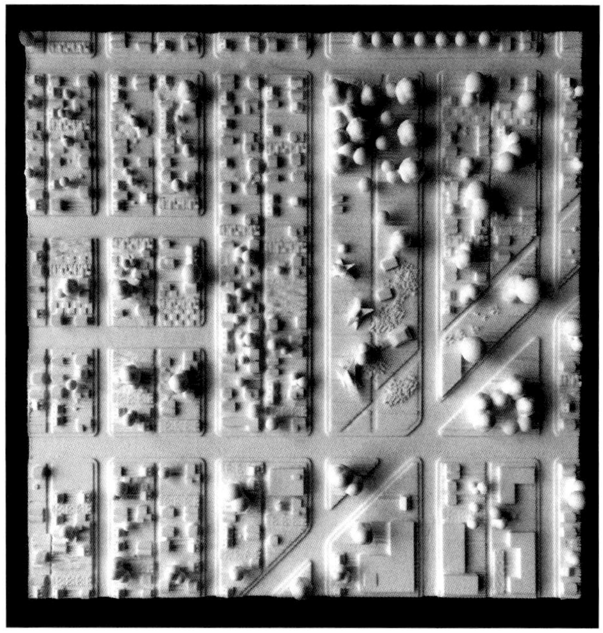

02. Successional Landscape

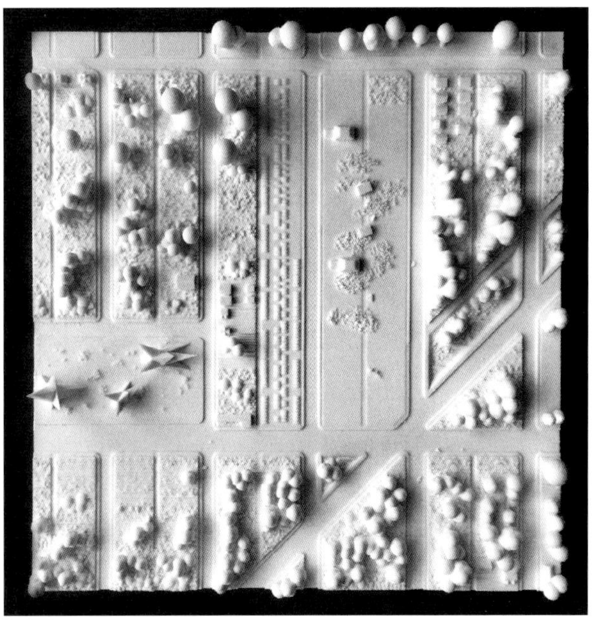

04. Successional + Events Landscape

05. Productive Landscape

Alternate futures for typical residential neighborhood lots in a depopulating city; how to reinscribe ecological vitality (newly green, still urbanized) and biodiversity across 139 square miles.

Detroit Future City

03. Green Mixed-Rise Residential

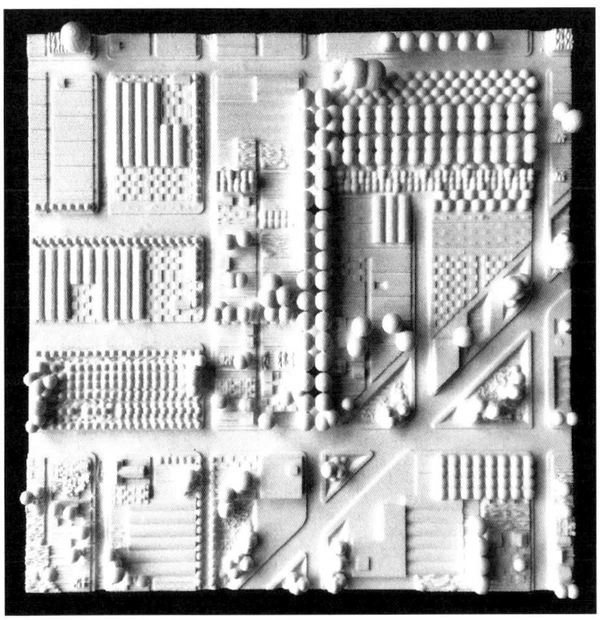

06. Cultivated Landscape

Conventional wisdom holds that plants sit on the landscape and wait for water, wait for sun, wait for spring, wait for everything to fall into place before they take their cue to grow... What if the landscape wasn't setting the stage for plants, but the plants were setting their own stage, green begetting green begetting green?

Hope Jahren

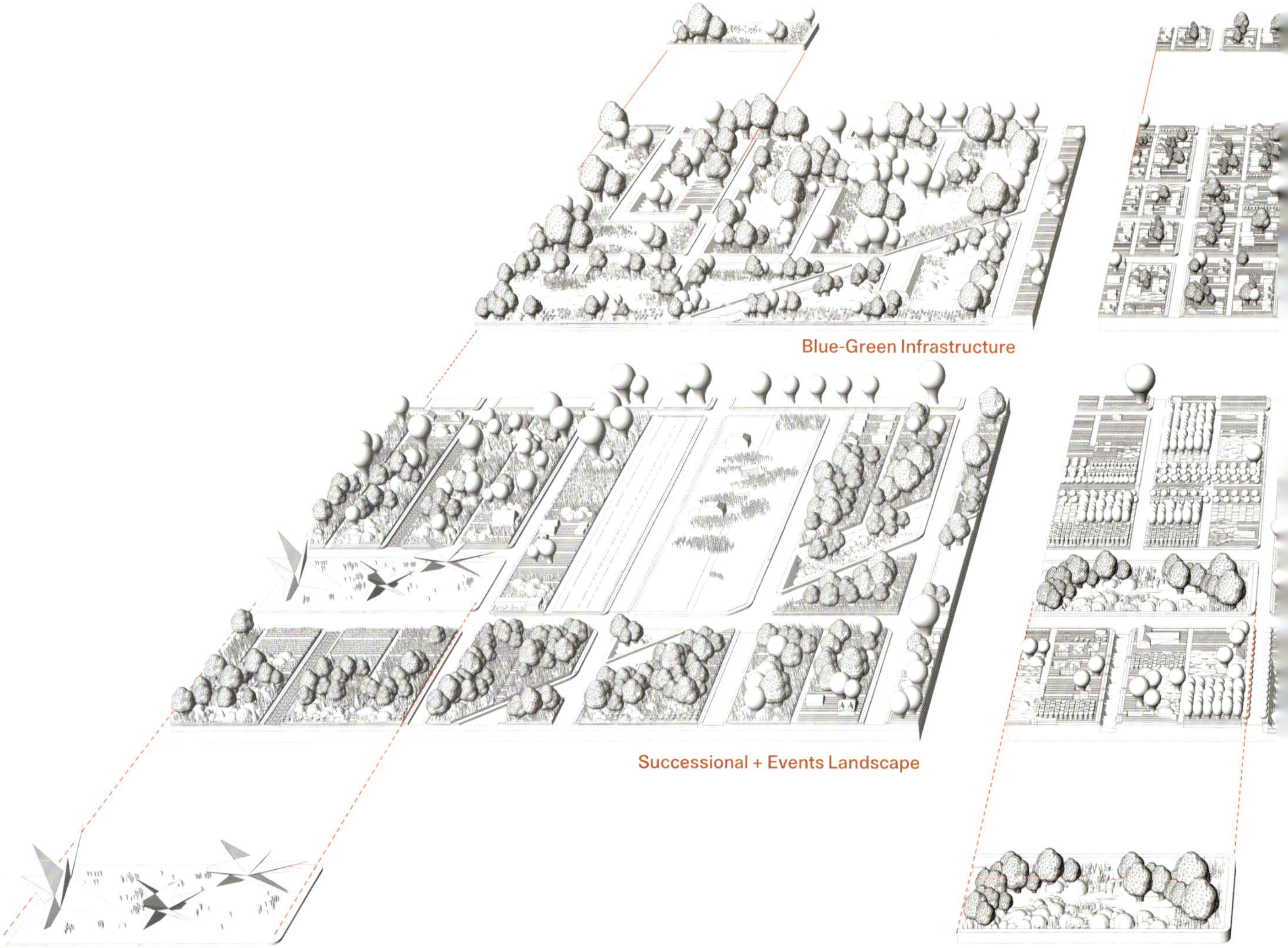

Reimagining newly productive urban land-scapes (cultivated, artful, water-absorbing, habitat-producing, densified, and green); new landscape-based forms of urban living.

Detroit Future City

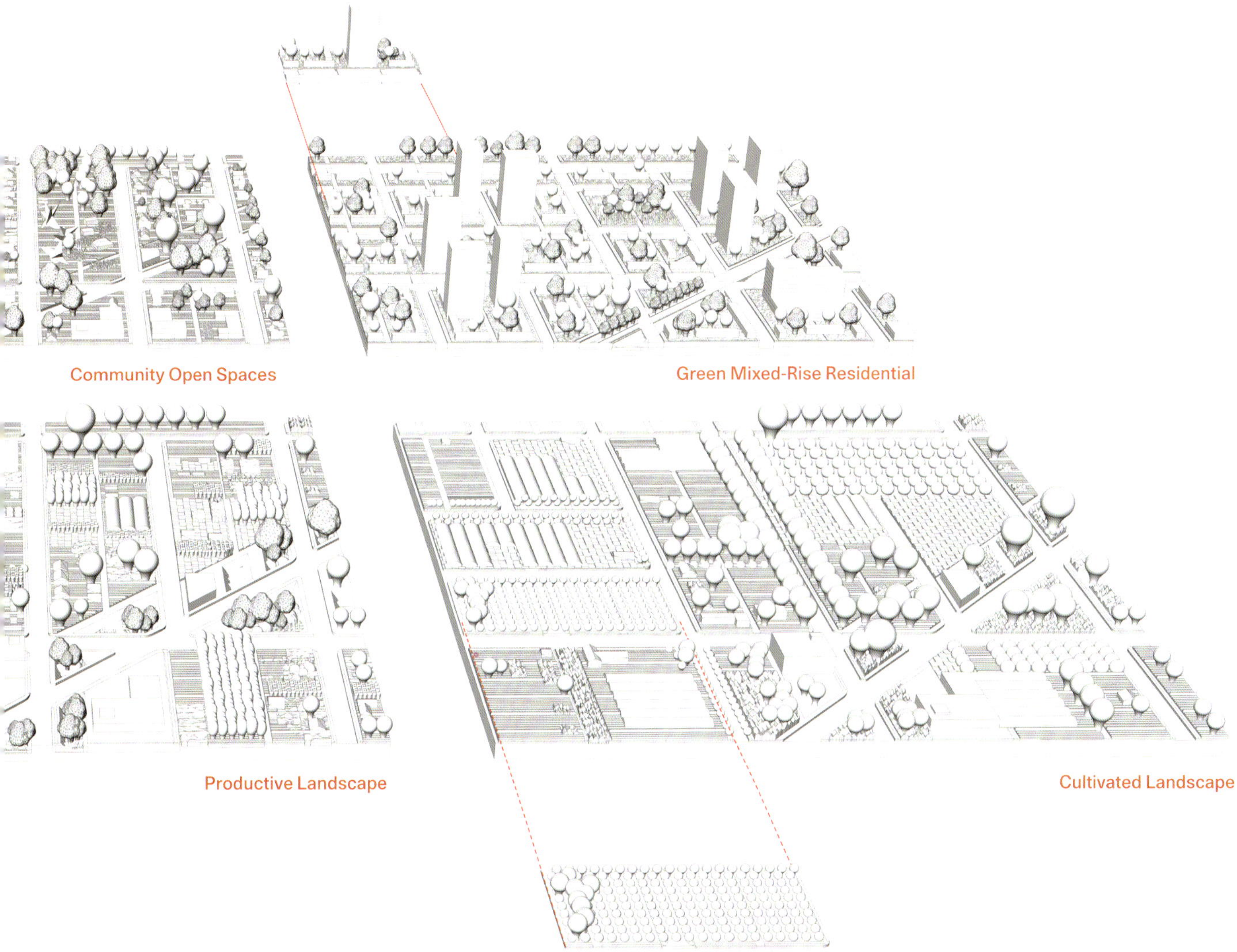

Community Open Spaces
Green Mixed-Rise Residential
Productive Landscape
Cultivated Landscape

Landscape
STAPLES
Jackson

People struggle everywhere, but it's interesting how the culture of a place factors into the particular type of struggle we are subjected to and the battles we choose. The couple I met in the Brightmoor neighborhood of Detroit had recently purchased a house from the Detroit land trust for $1,000. During my brief interaction with them, they found out that their water pipes had to be torn out and replaced, because they had lead in them. Later that spring they would begin their tomato farm on the small urban plot. Once they get the house livable, they will have a mortgage and rent-free home and land to farm to make a humble but low-pressure living. As others see the potential in this wasteland of burnt homes, the neighborhood will no doubt revitalize and thrive. The culture of this place is that if you are willing to put in the work, anything is possible.

Mike Belleme

Tigers
GRACO

"THEY TRIED TO
BURY US. THEY
DIDN'T KNOW
WE WERE SEEDS."

UNAUTHORIZED VEHICLES WILL BE TOWED AT THE OWNER'S EXPENSE AND LIABILITY
Light

Feeling the Heat: Transforming Cities for Healthy Climate Resilience

Nina-Marie Lister

In the Anthropocene, at the edge of climate disruption and impending biodiversity collapse, urban landscapes are at the nexus of mitigation, adaption, and transformation. Our cities are feeling the heat—literally and figuratively—but not evenly. At the same time, the benefits and bounty of biodiversity (the built-in, climate regulation services of nature) are disappearing before we can count, contain, and conserve them.[1] The interrelated effects of population growth (and decline), increasing migration, economic upheaval, coastal retreat, and civic unrest pose a mosaic of cumulative threats facing urban regions from continental coast to the interior. Both the culture and the nature of cities will and must shift to mitigate threats and adapt to these complex and mounting pressures. The environmental-ecological effects of climate change are becoming clear, from rising sea levels, coastal inundation, more frequent and severe storms, droughts and fires, all of which are exacerbating and accelerating the loss of nature's diversity, and its climate-balancing benefits. Less clear, but certainly potent and emerging are the concomitant social, political, and cultural effects of climate change—the impacts of which are discontinuous, disproportionate, punctuated, and political. Once again at the frontier of global change, North American cities face unprecedented potential for (r)evolution in pursuit of the resilience needed first to survive, and later, to thrive. In contemporary place-making initiatives in the American city, we find seeds of these potentials, whether lying dormant in declining places or (re)emerging in portraits of civic life. As our publics diversify, so too must the realms we inhabit for living, working and playing; our diverse and complex cities are the heartbeat of transformation to a more resilient and sustainable future.

Resilience

As more than half of Earth's people now live in cities, the landscapes most familiar and legible to us are urban[2]. By consequence, as a species we are losing our collective memory of the natural world and, with it, our variously embedded cultural understandings of and appreciations for how the ecological world works, including the innate resilience on which our societies implicitly rest. Yet the non-human living world is the best model of and for resilience, with a built-in capacity to self-regulate, absorb and, when necessary, adapt to the effects of disruption, disturbance, and change[3]. With the global shift to urban settlement and the accompanying increase in resources needed to fuel and sustain urban growth, urbanization unsurprisingly coincides with what is now broadly recognized as the climate crisis[4]. In this context, cities have become epicentres of climate action, underpinned by hope and despair, offering challenges and opportunities for relearning resilience, both in action and at rest.

From the design of policies and places alike, civic life and the public realm are windows into how we are learning—or not—to move from brittle resistance to flexible resilience in the face of unprecedented changes to the planetary systems that sustain life on earth. These changes are now documented in all mega- and major cities on earth: from record-breaking

heat waves and significant storm events to pestilence and predation, to deluge and drought, to famine and fire. At the center of every city's storm is the public realm: the heart of a city, revealing pivotal moments in urban life, death, and/or renewal. On this contemporary "civic stage," our local and collective struggles to build social and ecological resilience plays out: for equity, diversity, and inclusion to be seen and heard, to count and be counted, to counter a chaotic and messy world where social, economic, and environmental patterns are shifting.

Some cities and their publics resist, holding on to increasingly divisive and aging structures of colonial and corporate power while others bend, adapt, collectively opening to the diversity that will ultimately strengthen resilience. But the scale and extent of the twinned climate and biodiversity crises means active transition to resilience is now essential: we must learn to *change*, in order not to *be changed*, and thus, rendered ironic victims of our own planetary design[5].

Mitigation

How do we build resilience in the face of unprecedented planetary change? Modern industrial nations and their governments have advocated for mitigation strategies as the baseline intervention in climate change. Generally understood as human interventions to reduce the sources (e.g. fossil fuel emissions) and enhance sinks for sequestering greenhouse gases (e.g. maintaining soils and planting forests), mitigation has given rise to carbon offsets, carbon taxes, and investments in renewable energy[6]. But across the wealthy nations of the global North, mitigation efforts and investments are discontinuous, disingenuous, and dysfunctional. In the poorer nations of the global South, mitigation measures vary from untested and untapped to unfair, unreasonable, and unimaginable.

By 2019 the global, average, atmospheric CO_2 level reached 409.8 ppm (parts per million), which means that carbon dioxide levels today are higher than at any time in the last 800,000 years (i.e. well before modern humans were present, let alone widespread)[7]. In the waning days of 2020, we are drawing closer to a catastrophic threshold: a 1.5°C increase in average surface temperature at which point CO_2 levels will trigger irreversible changes to planetary boundaries. These changes include unpredictable impacts on the regulating cycles of water, carbon, and nutrients, affecting atmospheric and ocean currents,

plankton production, soil health, fresh water reserves, pollination, and seed viability (among other impacts)[8]. These changes have already triggered more frequent and stronger storm events, glacial melting, ocean acidification, continental drought, fire, and sea level rise. In even the least-worst scenarios, it is clear that we need a diversity of strategies and approaches to cope with such changes that mark the end of the temperate and predictable climate that brought human life to its zenith. Mitigation of carbon production alone will not ameliorate the crisis. Once we pass the threshold at which global carbon storage in the polar icecaps, sea ice, and peat bogs has been unlocked, positive feedback loops will further exacerbate the pace and amplify the scale of planetary warming. Along with these cumulative impacts will come devastating effects to most life as we know it.

To date, global climate actions sanctioned and led by the United Nations and its member states have relied principally on mitigation efforts to reduce and/or remove greenhouse gas emissions from the atmosphere. More recently, climate action has included adaption efforts to adjust systems and societies to withstand the increasingly unavoidable impacts of climate change[9]. Yet these two strategies are falsely polarized. Separating mitigation from adaptation is counterproductive and has led to the mistaken belief that effective action on climate change means pursuing *either* mitigation *or* adaptation[10]. Rather, it is increasingly clear that we need both strategies and more—urgently.

Adaptation

Cities are focal points for climate impacts as much as they are for the concentration of human social and economic energy, talent, and innovation. Municipal governments are often more agile in responding to crisis, and perhaps too with climate change. Urban regions and municipalities are increasingly likely to invest in their own resilience, creating social and economic policies that facilitate adaptive designs for climate change—new designs for climate-resilient, urban life from the ground up. Adaptive strategies are interventions that adjust natural and human systems in response to actual and expected climate change and its effects and that moderate harm and/or harness benefits and opportunities[11]. These include regional strategies and policies for working with and through climate change, deploying climate-adaptive infrastructure designs. To be

successful, climate-adaptive designs must be necessarily inclusive, equitable, and diverse regarding the people they engage, as much as regarding scale and approach.

At the regional scale, nature-based solutions are adaptive strategies grounded in connected biodiverse habitats, encompassing both natural and naturalized landscapes, from protected areas and natural heritage systems to recreational trails and open spaces to public parks and gardens[12]. Locally, purpose-built green infrastructure augments climate adaptation: ameliorating urban heat island effects, stormwater flooding, and severe weather through the addition of district renewable energy, sustainable (certified "green") architecture, diverse street trees, porous pavements, green roofs, wildlife passages, connected parks systems, and so on[13]. Integral to the fabric of living landscapes, adaptive green infrastructure can remediate and restore the benefits of nature in the city: connections to nature are now understood to be vital to human physical and mental health, as well as to emotional and cultural well-being[14]. In addition to providing naturalized places to recreate, exercise, relax, and recharge, integrating nature into the urban landscape provides important benefits not only to humans but also to wildlife, including cooling, shading, pollination, carbon capture and storage, oxygen production, improved water quality and infiltration, flood management, and food production through urban farming, foraging, and seed collection.

Repositioned as critical infrastructural investments that deliver essential services, nature-based solutions broadly, and green infrastructure designs specifically, may become integral components in the emerging Green New Deal and "building back better," post-pandemic and on the doorstep of the climate crisis. Never before has the value of the public realm, through parks, open spaces, and access to nature been as critical for human health and well-being. Taken together, collective strategies of adaptive redesign must enable planning and building livable, equitable, sustainable cities that can weather the coming storms as much as provide joyful, accessible places for collective innovation and renewal. The co-benefits of this synergy can build urban resilience through restored biodiversity, improved human physical health and mental well-being, and a transition to new, green economies.[15]

Transformation

How do we imagine a future that has no precedent in our past? Our histories are shared in poetry, songs and stories, artworks and photographs, grounded in landscapes and places that may be, in one generation, irrevocably altered or lost altogether. Our futures are imagined, speculated and visualized through media that help us "see" differently. Photography is powerful in this respect, at once reflecting the past while projecting the potential of a place—in so doing, it is both mirror and window. In photographing urban spaces in transition, we gain insights into alternative futures, to the power and potential of places, and ultimately to the transformation necessary to thrive in the coming world. So, what will we see ahead?

Transformation is necessary adaptation to an unknown state, to a new world that is unfolding fast and for which we may—or not—fit. Climate change, biodiversity loss, and the global pandemic have collectively and dramatically exposed vulnerabilities and revealed social-ecological systems complexities that include the interrelationships and intersectionality of health, food production, global supply chains, habitat destruction, energy, transportation, and so on. Such complex issues relate to scale, distribution, and critical infrastructure needs. As with pipelines, roads, sewers, and bridges (our conventional grey infrastructure of the past), biodiversity and living habitats, including urban nature, are increasingly recognized as components of critical infrastructure, all of which have embedded co-benefits for climate regulation and human health and well-being. When reframed as essential services and positioned as critical green infrastructure, biodiversity and living habitats can unlock significant opportunities for urban sustainability through mitigation, adaptation, and, potentially, when needed, transformation. Addressing the intersection of the climate and biodiversity crises through making investments in nature-based solutions generally, and green infrastructure specifically, builds not only adaptive but *transformative* capacity. Cities of the future will need to harness the co-benefits of nature's biodiversity and human health and well-being through coupling or "stacking" civic programs with green infrastructure in urban spaces. Imagine complete streets as green streets, where pedestrians take priority, parks prevail, and the public realm dominates; where buildings provide more power than they consume, food is grown on roofs and terraces, parks provide healing,

teaching and learning, and urban forests regenerate nutrients, pollinate, infiltrate, and oxygenate. This is not utopia but climate-adaptive planning and design for resilience: the only viable strategy for surviving—and thriving in the coming age.

Climate-adaptive resilient designs can transform places: from architecture to place-making, from the site to the region, cities must physically and accessibly connect people to the sustaining power of nature, not only for its benefits and services to people, but also for its inherent value. In a warmer, more volatile future, cities will only thrive with nature in place, where green infrastructure is embedded in building codes and zoning, as a standard part of city building in every community. But there is no leader, no agency or government alone that will meet the complex challenges of mitigation, adaptation, and transformation for climate resilience. Our future rests in cities and their publics, collaborating across divides with many and varied approaches. Cities are where decisions are made about the land and how we live. The work towards transformation demands diverse communities of progressive urban leaders, activists, and place-makers: it is urgent work for many hands and voices that transcend disciplines, borders, and industries. And it is public work—an essential service for our children and the creatures of the earth that sustains us.

Notes

1 IPBES 2019: *Global Assessment Report on Biodiversity and Ecosystem Services*. https://ipbes.net/global-assessment
2 Ellis, E.C., 2011. Anthropogenic Transformation of the Terrestrial Biosphere. *Proceedings of the Royal Society A: Mathematical, Physical and Engineering Science*, 369(1938): p. 1010–1035.
3 Rockström, Johan; et al. (2009). "Planetary Boundaries: Exploring the Safe Operating Space for Humanity". *Ecology and Society*. 14 (2). doi:10.5751/ES-03180-140232.
4 Seto, K.C. *et al* 2012. Global Forecasts of Urban Expansion to 2030 and Direct Impacts on Biodiversity and Carbon Pools. *Proceedings of the National Academy of Science of the United States* 109, no. 40: 16083-16088.
5 Walker & Salt (2012) cited in Lister, N-M. (2016) Resilience Beyond Rhetoric in Urban Landscape Planning and Design. Chapter 13 in: F. Steiner, G. Thompson, & A.

Carbonell (eds) *Nature and Cities: The Ecological Imperative in Urban Planning and Design*. Lincoln Land Institute, pp 296–319.

6 Klein, R.J.T., S. Huq, F. Denton, T.E. Downing, R.G. Richels, J.B. Robinson, F.L. Toth, 2007: Inter-relationships between adaptation and mitigation. *Climate Change 2007: Impacts, Adaptation and Vulnerability. Contribution of Working Group II to the Fourth Assessment Report of the Intergovernmental Panel on Climate Change*, M.L. Parry, O.F. Canziani, J.P. Palutikof, P.J. van der Linden and C.E. Hanson, Eds., Cambridge University Press, Cambridge, UK, 745-777.

7 Lindsay, R. 2020. Climate Change: Atmospheric Carbon Dioxide. News Features. *NOAA Climate Watch*. https://www.climate.gov/news-features/understanding-climate/climate-change-atmospheric-carbon-dioxide

8 See Note 2.

9 IPCC, 2014: *Climate Change 2014: Synthesis Report. Contribution of Working Groups I, II and III to the Fifth Assessment Report of the Intergovernmental Panel on Climate Change* [Core Writing Team, R.K. Pachauri and L.A. Meyer (eds.)]. IPCC, Geneva, Switzerland, 151 pp. (See *AR5 Topic 4: Adaptation & Mitigation*: https://ar5-syr.ipcc.ch/topic_adaptation.php)

10 Suarez, I. 2020. Five Strategies that Achieve Climate Mitigation and Adaptation Simultaneously. *World Resources Institute*, online newsletter Febraury 10. https://www.wri.org/blog/2020/02/climate-change-mitigation-adaptation-strategies and World Resources Institute, 2020. *Global Commission on Adaption*. https://www.wri.org/our-work/project/global-commission-adaptation

11 See Note 8

12 See e.g. Cohen-Sacham, 2016. *A Nature-Based Solutions Framework*. IUCN. https://www.iucn.org/theme/ecosystem-management/our-work/a-global-standard-nature-based-solutions and European Commission, 2020. Draft EU Biodiversity Strategy for 2030: Bringing nature back into our lives. https://www.arc2020.eu/wp-content/uploads/2020/05/Biodiversity-Strategy_draft_200423_ARC2020.pdf

13 See e.g. *ICLEI Resilient Cities*: http://resilient-cities.iclei.org/ and Silverstein, Y. & Green, J. 2019. *Guide to Green Infrastructure Practice*. American Society of Landscape Architects. https://www.asla.org/greeninfrastructure.aspx

14 Beatley, T. (2017). Commentary: Biophilic Cities and Healthy Societies. *Urban Planning*. 2(4), 1–4. See also examples in the Biophilic Cities Network: https://www.biophiliccities.org/journals

15 Lister, N-M. (in press) Activating healthy urban landscapes: improving human wellbeing through exposure to nature in parks and urban landscape design. *Socio-ecological Perspectives*.

Boston, Massachusetts

A city of history on the edge of the Atlantic, Boston is a cultural, educational, and research center that still struggles with its identity and with transformation. Rapidly redeveloping in the face of climate change and the very present effects of flooding, more culturally diverse than ever (with its longstanding, racially and culturally diverse but underrepresented populations living alongside some of the most entrenched White people), it wrestles with how climatic, economic, and cultural changes will influence the lives of all of those who are here. Who (or what) might displace them? Who will live in the expanding city, where social, environmental, and economic currents are deeply and inextricably intertwined, and point toward uncertain futures?

Atlantic Ocean
Somerville
Chelsea
Winthrop
East
Boston
Cambridge
Back Bay
South Boston
Boston Harbor
Brookline
Roxbury
Massachusetts Bay
Dorchester
Codman
Square
Roslindale
Quincy Bay
Hingham Bay
Quincy
Milton
Dedham

It was a windy night, and before my retina registered anything, I was smitten by a feeling of utter happiness: my nostrils were hit by what to me has always been its synonym, the smell of freezing seaweed. For some people, it's freshly cut grass or hay; for others, Christmas scents of conifer needles and tangerines. For me, it's freezing seaweed…

Joseph Brodsky

CINER

Street Cleaning
Resident Permit Parking

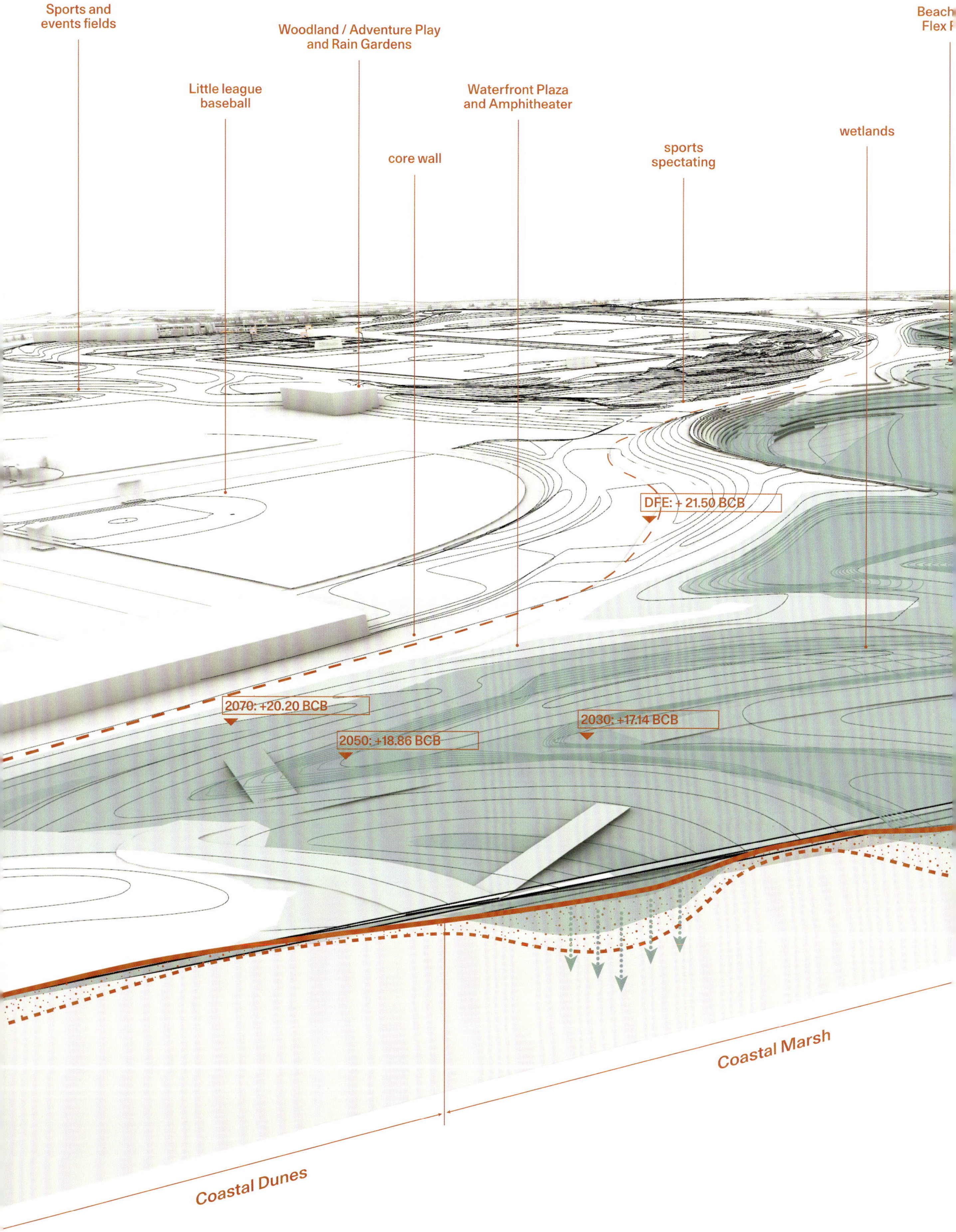
Sports and events fields
Woodland / Adventure Play and Rain Gardens
Little league baseball
Waterfront Plaza and Amphitheater
core wall
sports spectating
wetlands
DFE: + 21.50 BCB
2070: +20.20 BCB
2050: +18.86 BCB
2030: +17.14 BCB
Coastal Marsh
Coastal Dunes

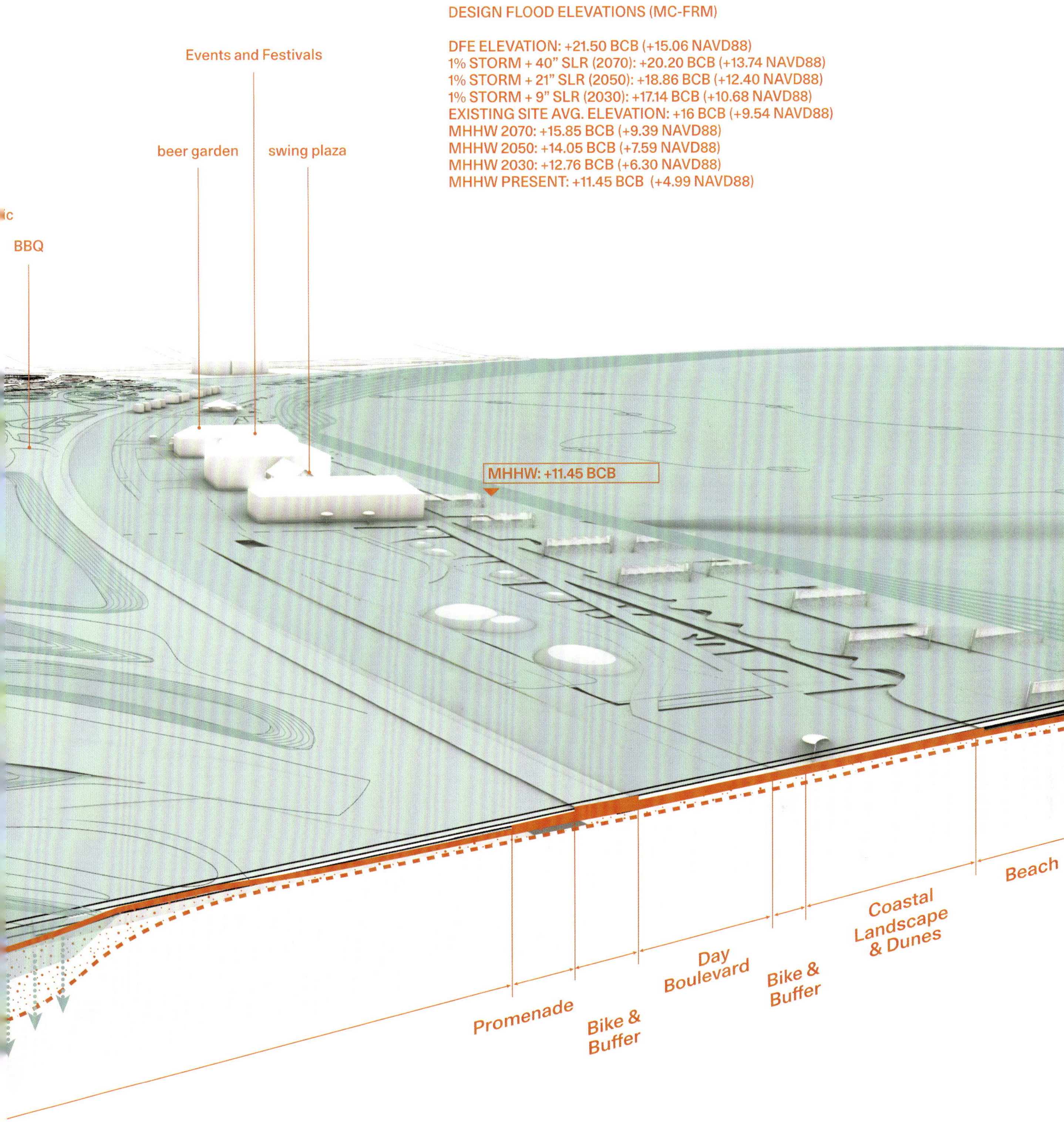

Can increased flooding and impending climate disaster spur new approaches to inclusivity and open space? A public park reimagined with dynamic coastal ecologies and new activity areas that invite a fuller range of urban dwellers to the harbor.

Moakley Park, South Boston

We have some ideas about building one good, decent baseball field with sports turf and then there'd be open space for something else. They could use the other fields for something else, as long as we had a decent field to play on. You wouldn't believe how many games are cancelled because of the puddles all over the place.

Local Resident

United Rentals
United Rentals
United Rentals
United Rentals
United Rentals

United Rentals
United Rentals
United Rentals
JLG LIFT
LIFT

METROPOLITAN STORAGE WAREHOUSE
FIRE PROOF

When a place is constantly in flux, it's easy for it to go unnoticed. Even extreme shifts can be adapted to and adopted as a new normal. There are thresholds though, a precipice where small incremental changes topple over into an undeniably new reality. Several neighborhoods in Boston feel that way. Balanced on the edge of a new reality. Waiting for the other shoe to drop. Rising waters, shifts in demographics, fates intertwined. What can people do, powerless to forces greater than themselves, but go on with their lives?

Mike Belleme

The 'life of the city' can be reduced neither to the rational functionality of the modern city nor to the nostalgic and colorful pastiches of the past. The challenge for urbanists is how to combine rationality with imagination, the prosaic with the dream world, the planned with the unexpected—the city as the site of multiple representations and multiple desires.

Mohsen Mostafavi

PLAZA
WINTER
FEST
COMMON
SPACES

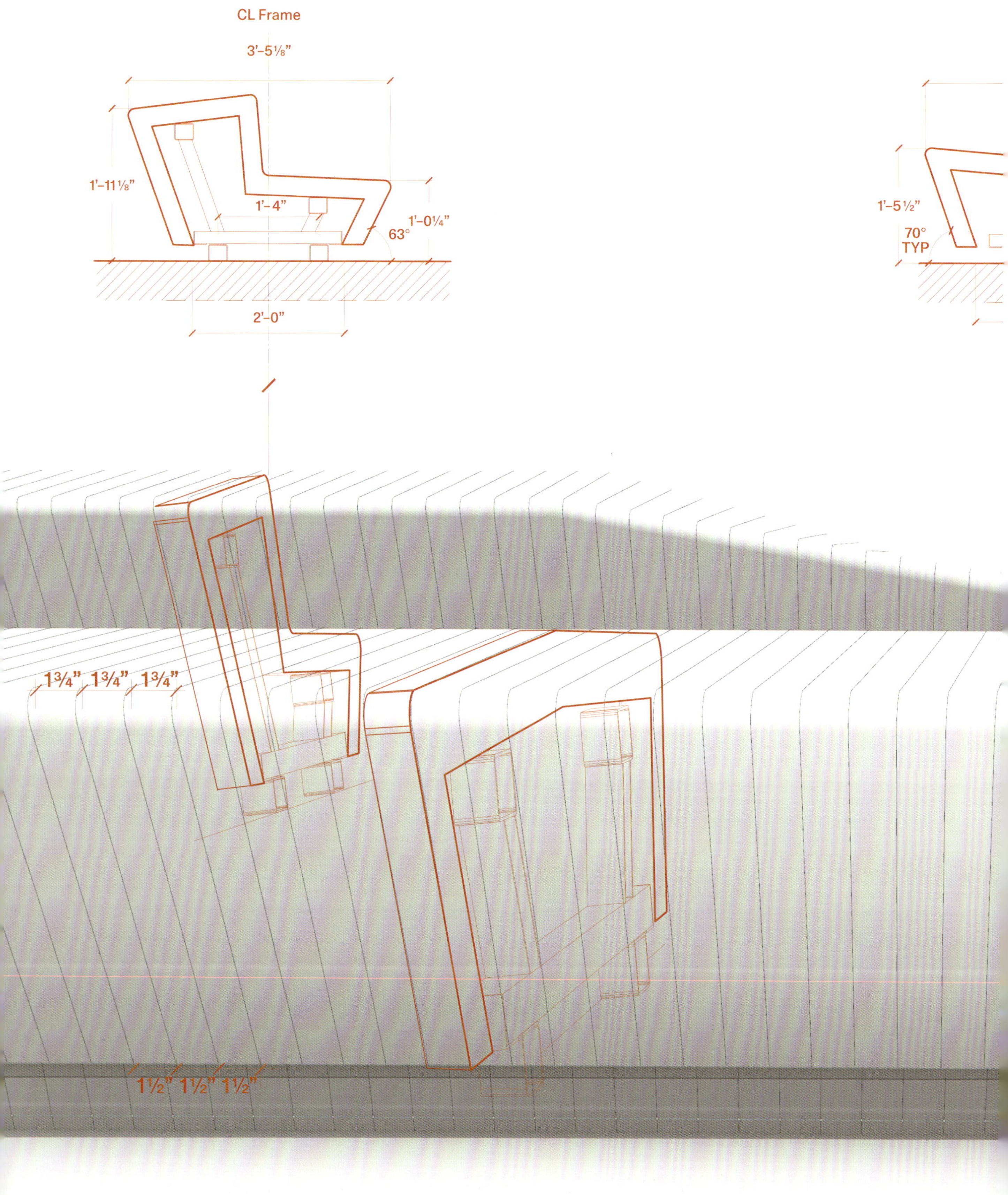
CL Frame
3'-5⅛"
1'-11⅛"
1'-4"
1'-0¼"
63°
2'-0"
1'-5½"
70° TYP
1¾" 1¾" 1¾"
1½" 1½" 1½"

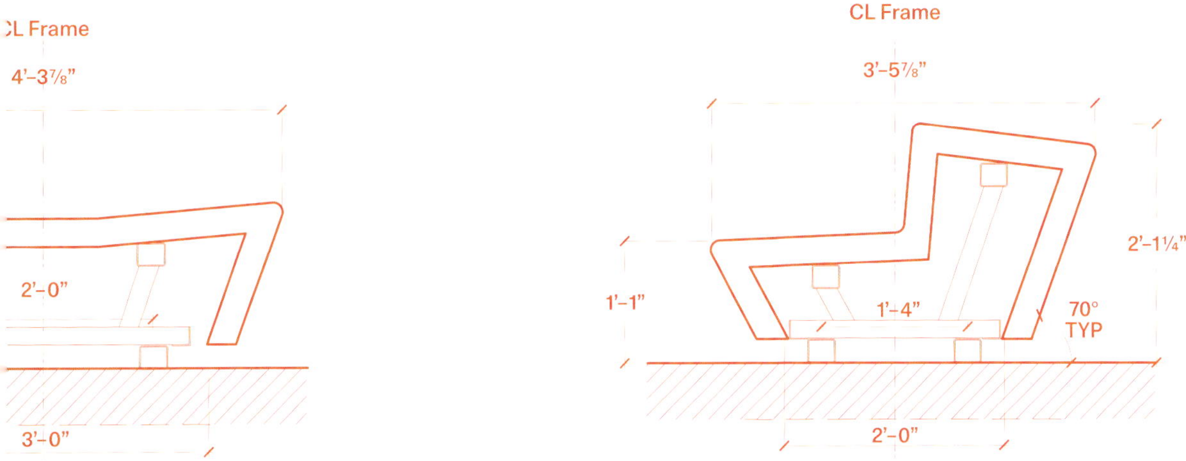

Distinct sitting profiles—tuned to a variety of body types and reclining/lounging positions—are morphed from one to the other, creating smooth transitions and unique bench form. What's your pleasure? Alone or in a group? Cross-legged or straight upright? Lying down or with a friend in your lap?

Science Center Plaza, Harvard University, Cambridge

What Was, What Is, and What Ought To Be: Three Reflections on the Relationship Between Photography and Design

Sara Zewde

In her book *The Eye Is a Door*, Anne Whiston Spirn profoundly makes the case for the inextricable nature of seeing and thinking, through the exploration of etymology:

> *To see* is the root of idea, linguistically and literally: the word *idea* comes from the Greek ιδειν, to see… […] *Image*, from the Latin *imāgo*, meaning imitation, appearance, thought, or idea, is the root of imagination… *To speculate*, from the Latin *speculārī*, to watch or observe, is to theorize… […] Implicit in this etymology is the belief that the world is the source of ideas, which are drawn out through visual perception in a dialogue between self and surroundings.

Prompted by Anne Spirn's proposition, and the pairing of Stoss and Belleme's works, I find myself reflecting on the relationship between photography and design in three ways: what was, what is, and what ought to be.

What Was

In neuroscience, many theories hold that identity is formed by one's memory. Suppose you sustain an injury to your brain and lose your memory. So, too, is your sense of self-identity and consciousness as a person as having been shaped by past experiences. Philosophers such as the seventeenth century's John Locke profess that identity is dependent upon a "continued consciousness," and that memory and meaning are formed by a process of reflection on patterns over time.

Similarly, a sense of place or identity in an urban landscape is contingent upon resonance with its past. In this way, the documentary nature of photography and its ability to capture *what was* can be a pivotal tool for designers in the process of sensing, and thus designing for, the continued consciousness of a place. Photographs are evidentiary material for reading histories, and as such, are indexes of place identities, rich with creative departures for designs that are in dialogue with the past. Documentary photography such as the work of Belleme, then, offers a means to identify emergent patterns, make comparisons and connections across time and scales, and form insights on the meaning of a place. These views onto *what was* are critical for a designer such as Reed, in the careful insertion of a contemporary landscape in the myriad historical dynamics that continue to shape the city.

What Is

Beyond what was, the photograph is also a lens onto *what is*. The city, as Teju Cole writes, is "what is everywhere but is everywhere slightly different." Photography is a valuable tool for seeing the city, in all its distinct banality. The media with which landscape architects work is really this banal stuff of the city—its benches, paving, trees, street lights, and more. Photography is a prompt for discerning the poetics of quotidian city life. It is a stop-frame on what can be the numbing relentlessness of everyday life, calling attention to the shades of these urban textures that are

What Was: photography is a pivotal tool for designers in the process of sensing what was

generative for the creative practice of designing them.

A quantum reality underlies the dialogue between Reed and Belleme's work as presented in *Mise-en Scène*. For instance, a construction drawing of a bench, presented alongside a photograph of two people interacting on a bench, is a proposition that the urban landscape is more than a statis scene. It, too, is an actor on the world that is. It suggests that the bench is an actor within a universe of forces that influence these two people to engage in this place. For a photograph to pause on a moment in time within this milieu, prompts reflection on the forces that underlie the world that we live in, calling attention to the urban landscapes that shape our lives. The dialogue between photography and design, as both an analytical and speculative practice, helps us to understand the interconnectedness of things, lending insights as testimony into *what is.*

What Ought To Be

Both photography and design are acts of shaping how someone views the world. It's an incredible power to wield and one that is inherently propositional. Frederick Douglass, one of the first critical theorists of photography, is considered the most photographed person of the nineteenth century. Once enslaved, Douglass did not coincidentally achieve this distinction. Rather, he actively sought out opportunities to be photographed, convinced that photographs were able to reveal his very humanity, which in turn could energize abolitionist movements.

On December 3, 1861, in a lecture entitled *Pictures and Progress* at Tremont Temple in Boston, Massachusetts, Douglass professes: "Poets, prophets and reformers are all picture-makers—and this ability is the secret of their power and of their achievements. They see what ought to be by the reflection of what is, and endeavor to remove the contradiction." Through the triangulation of what is what was, and what *ought to be*, photography and design prompt one to indulge in the kind of utopian imagination necessary to energizing activism. There are striking similarities in the analytical endeavors of remembering the past, analyzing the present, and imagining a future. What worked?

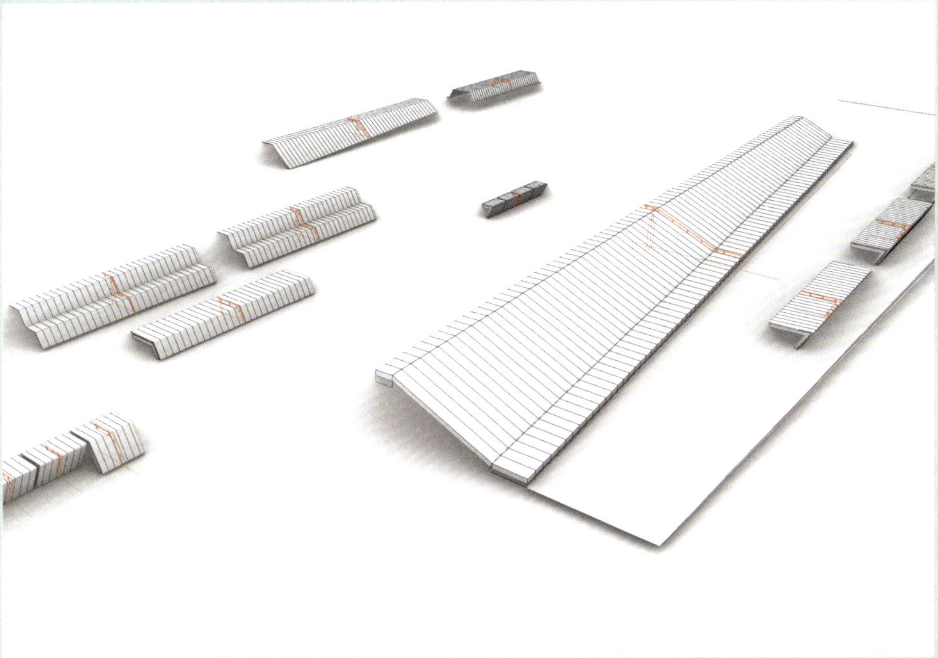

What Is: the urban landscape is an actor in the world that is

What didn't? What is working? What isn't working? What shall we conserve, destroy, and build in our new world? And, how do we advocate for it? The imaginary worlds shaped by the acts of making photographs and designing landscapes bring focus on *what ought to be.*

Afterword
Mike Belleme

The process of making this work was one of semi-aimless wandering. I never really knew what I was looking for but just had to trust that something would stop me and demand my attention, and it always did. Most of the time, it was a subtle pull of curiosity, as though I didn't really know if it would make a good picture, but it was of enough interest to try. There were a few instances though that hit me like a frying pan across the head. Things I couldn't have ignored if I'd tried. The best example of this was in Green Bay as I was driving along in a neighborhood and looked to my right to see the man sitting in his yard watering his lawn. The positioning of the hose and the stream of water were just so. The image was already composed. I saw the photo, clear as day, in that fleeting moment as I passed by. I swerved off the road, made my way back to the man, and asked to make the picture. It was the easiest of all of the photos to make. The picture already existed, just needed someone to happen upon it. I had a similar reaction when I came upon the man standing in a parking lot outside of his apartment in East Boston. He was smoking a cigarette and drinking coffee from a mug, backlit by the morning sun hitting nothing in the scene but the top of his head and the smoke from the cigarette. Both scenes were a mix of public and private moments. The smoker, so domestic with his mug, basketball shorts, and Crocs, and the mundane act of lawn maintenance on public display to anyone willing to notice.

Afterword
Chris Reed

Over and over, I find myself in muddy terrain or murky waters, at the center of passionate and sometimes heated public conversations—with the people and forces struggling to re-shape the world around them, or just trying to persist. In this work, we try to bring forward invisible people and forces, to give space and time to the hidden, buried, and vulnerable especially, and to find moments of joy and pleasure and intimacy and beauty that are meaningful to them. Momentarily, we bring something of ourselves to this work, too—our training and life experiences, our perspectives on design and culture, and our empathy—to mix with the backgrounds and folks and stuff of a particular place and time to create distinct expressions rooted in the stories and histories and people we work with. Ultimately, though, this process of learning, imagining, and projecting culminates the moment we walk away from these projects, when people, time, and entropy take over and just do what they will do. This is when the richness of the work begins, the moment when the *mise-en-scène* once again becomes scene. What will happen next is the question both of the moment and of our time.

Contributors

Chris Reed is founder and Design Director of Stoss Landscape Urbanism, a design and strategic planning practice in Boston and Los Angeles whose work focuses on the revitalization of landscapes and cities. He also serves as Professor in Practice of Landscape Architecture and is the Ecologies Domain Head for the Master of Design Studies Program at the Harvard Graduate School of Design. He is a leading disciplinary voice on issues related to climate adaptation, racial and social equity, urban landscape, and the sociability of cities.

Mike Belleme is a freelance photographer based in Asheville, North Carolina. His work ranges from long-form documentary projects to assignment-based editorial work, photojournalism, and portraiture. His practice involves photographing from a space of emotional availability and vulnerability and exploring themes involving connection and disconnection from that space.

Mimi Zeiger is a Los Angeles-based critic and curator. She was co-curator of the U.S. Pavilion for the 2018 Venice Architecture Biennale and curator of *Soft Schindler* at the MAK Center for Art and Architecture.

De Nichols is a communications designer and artist-activist who serves as the Social Impact Design Principal of Civic Creatives in St. Louis. Her work champions the power of design and storytelling to inspire and equip change makers to protest social injustices and design civic solutions for progressive change across American communities.

Julia Czerniak is associate dean and professor of architecture at Syracuse University where she teaches on landscape theory and criticism. Her work focuses on the physical and cultural potentials of urban landscapes.

Nina-Marie Lister is an ecologist and planner, Graduate Program Director and Associate Professor in the School of Urban + Regional Planning at Ryerson University in Toronto. She is the founder and director of the Ecological Design Lab at Ryerson University.

Sara Zewde is founding principal of Studio Zewde, a design firm in New York City practicing landscape architecture, urbanism, and public art. The studio is devoted to exploring the "aesthetics of being" and creating enduring places where people belong. She also serves as Assistant Professor of Practice at Harvard University Graduate School of Design.

Acknowledgements
Chris Reed

This project took many forms before it became the one you see: it's been a number of years in the making and comes from the collective efforts and inputs of so many. It started with casual but focused conversations with some long-standing, close colleagues in unusual settings: Elizabeth Meyer in a Los Angeles cafe, Julia Czerniak in a studio at the American Academy in Rome, Michael Jakob on a visit to my Boston office, Charles Waldheim in a bar or two in Cambridge. Through these discussions, the project emerged in a few different forms. One of these previous versions, tentatively titled *WORK-LIFE,* privileged the inner workings of Stoss and was very "inside-baseball" for designers. But it seemed too self-centered, too much about us, and too much about us talking to other designers—rather than about the broader social, environmental, and cultural currents that shape our world, shape us as people, and shape our work. Beth, Julia, Michael, and Charles were instrumental in helping to sharpen my focus; our conversations were impactful and are deeply appreciated.

E. Scott Mitchell, who was working for Stoss at the time and who is now pursuing a PhD at the University of Virginia, helped shape the photographic approach and search for photographers with me. Sadly (for us!) he left for school just as Mike was getting going. And Siena Scarff productively probed the project as the photographs were coming in and drawings were developed—ultimately helping to shape the nature of the book itself.

Patsy Baudoin edited and crafted the words as much as Benjamin Rasmussen helped me and Mike edit images and craft photographic story-lines. Both were sharp, no-nonsense, and invaluable.

Sonny Xu, William Baumgardner, Sophie Elias, Koby Moreno, and Petra Geiger all assisted with critical components of the project along the way. Amy Whitesides, Joonyon Kim, and Petra have all stepped up at Stoss in recent years to both transform the practice and to carry bigger loads and responsibilities, opening up time and brain-space for me to develop this work. Adam Michaels, Shannon Harvey, and Marina Kitchen at IN-FO.CO became wonderful partners as they honed our rough materials into a simple and elegant presentation. Gordon Goff, Alejandro Guzman-Avila, and their team at ORO Editions were terrific supporters all along—Gordon pressed me to do this project for a couple of years before I finally gave in! I appreciate his persistence and am grateful for everyone's contributions.

Of course, the many people I and the folks at Stoss have come to know over the past 20 years have been generous with their input and willingness to share their lives and experiences with us. We benefit from a wonderful array of clients that simply want to do good work, and from various stakeholders, members of the public, and team members that both inform and help to realize these projects—both in those cities represented here, and beyond. I appreciate each and every one of you.

When it became time to get serious and turn this into a book, Alysoun Wright stepped in and took over in the most comprehensive, professional, and thoughtful ways. She was fearless in gently pressing contributors, organizing schedules and deliverables, working with IN-FO.CO and ORO, getting permissions, finishing drawings, endlessly revising, and in keeping me focused and on track. I couldn't ask for a better or steadier right hand.

A huge shout-out to my writers and contributors—Mimi and De, who were first in (!) and Julia, Sara, and Nina-Marie, all of whom shared their time and many probing conversations. The care and craft and thoughtfulness of their essays are remarkable, I especially appreciate the ways in which their own voices and projects are extended through these efforts. And I am humbled and thankful that each of them took part and contributed something of themselves in some of the most trying months of the pandemic.

Most importantly, I want to thank Mike for his deeply personal and professional contributions here. In our first call, he explained to me that I had mistaken him for an architectural photographer—that there were people who did photography of projects like ours, and he wasn't that kind of photographer! He learned quickly that this was exactly why I called him. Ever since, we've been engaged in an unfolding and evolving conversation about cities, people, our professional influences and interests, and our own personal lives. We've become both collaborators and friends, the kind where thoughtful silence and reflection is as meaningful as energized conversation. I emerge with new eyes, new perspectives—even on places I thought I knew so well.

Finally, love to my family—Paige, Silas, Jasper, and Etta. You each allow me—challenge me, even—to see the world in new ways. Thanks for your patience, your support, and the joy each of you brings to life.

Acknowledgements
Mike Belleme

First and foremost I have to give the deepest of gratitude to my collaborator, Chris Reed. The amount of trust he put in me on this project boggles my mind. He introduced me to a whole new way of viewing my surroundings and shared his knowledge of the cities and thoughtfulness around the complexity of social and environmental conditions specific to each of them. I never have and perhaps never will again get this combination of creative freedom and resources and time to work on something. I also want to thank the rest of the Stoss team who have been incredibly helpful and supportive. Specifically, Scott Mitchell, William Baumgardner, and Alysoun Wright for their input and organization and Petra Geiger for being the voice of reason. Special thanks to Benjamin Rasmussen for helping us struggle through the difficult decisions on the chopping block. Thanks to the folks at IN-FO.CO and ORO for refining our vision and bringing it to life. Thank you to all of the amazing people who shared moments of your life with me in LA, Galveston, St. Louis, Green Bay, Ann Arbor, Detroit, and Boston. Thanks to my wife, Kristen for tolerating the extensive travel schedule and for all of her love and support, and my family for their unceasing support of my creative endeavors. Because I never was officially schooled as a photographer, I want to acknowledge at least a few of the folks helped me along the way. My brother, Justin, for helping me get some of my first clients and enabling me to take the leap into freelance photography. My dad for getting me my first camera and teaching me the basics. Jon Menick for all of the energy he put into my development as a photographer and as a friend. Bryan Derballa for introducing me to the world of photography that I know now and the community that I cherish. And to the many others that have offered time, knowledge, and friendship along the way.

Credits

Setting the Stage: The Social Lives of Urban Landscapes

Social Ecologies, Eda U. Gerstacker Grove, University of Michigan, Ann Arbor, Michigan, USA, drawing © Chris Reed and Stoss Inc.

Cole, Teju. *Blind Spot*. First ed. New York: Random House, 2017.

From the Good Looking Out Series, B/W Silver Gelatin "Untitled" Location: Newark, NJ Date: 1995, photograph by Jules Allen, © Jules Allen

Ladies Having Dinner, photograph by Herman Hertzberger, © Herman Hertzberger

Harvard Science Center Plaza Benches, Harvard University, Cambridge, Massachusetts, USA, drawing © Chris Reed and Stoss Inc.

Plan of portion of park system from Common to Franklin Park: including Charles River Basin, Charlesbank, Commonwealth Avenue, Back Bay Fens, Muddy River Improvement, Leverett Park, Jamaica Park, Arborway and Arnold Arboretum, 1894, map by Olmsted, Olmsted, and Eliot, courtesy of Norman B. Leventhal Map & Education Center at the Boston Public Library

Boys picking over garbage dump, 1909, photograph by Lewis Wickes Hine, courtesy of Library of Congress, Prints & Photographs Division, National Child Labor Committee Collection, [reproduction number, e.g., LC-USZ62-108765]

From the Good Looking Out Series, B/W Silver Gelatin "Untitled" Location: Harlem, NY Date: 1992, photograph by Jules Allen, © Jules Allen

Landscape, Minneapolis, 1974, photograph by Frank Gohlke, © Frank Gohlke 1974

Model of Galveston Seawall Central Galveston Island, Texas, USA, model © Chris Reed and Stoss Inc.

Map: City of Boston, Boston, Massachusetts, USA, drawing © Chris Reed and Stoss Inc.

Clearing Winter Storm, Yosemite National Park, California, c. 1937, photograph by Ansel Adams, © The Ansel Adams Publishing Rights Trust Courtesy of The Ansel Adams Publishing Rights Trust

Nickel Tailings #34, Sudbury, Ontario, 1996, photograph by Edward Burtynsky © Edward Burtynsky, courtesy Weinstein Hammons Gallery, Minneapolis / Nicholas Metivier Gallery, Toronto

Marias River Drainage and Pivot Irrigator, Loma Area, MT 1995, photograph by Alex S. MacLean, © Alex S. MacLean / Landslides Aerial Photography

Adams, Robert, William. Jenkins, and International Museum of Photography at George Eastman House. New Topographics: Photographs of a Man-altered Landscape. Rochester, N.Y.: International Museum of Photography at George Eastman House, 1975.

Dwyer, James. "Life Uncurated." The New York Times. April 29, 2018, sec. Scenes Unseen: The Summer of '78.

Los Angeles

Map: City of Los Angeles, Los Angeles, California, USA, drawing © Chris Reed and Stoss Inc.

Varnelis, Kazys. *The Infrastructural City : Networked Ecologies in Los Angeles*. Barcelona ; New York : [Los Angeles] : [New York]: Actar; The Los Angeles Forum for Architecture and Urban Design; The Network Architecture Lab, Graduate School of Architecture, Planning and Preservation, Columbia University, 2008.

LA2 Freeway, Frogtown- Elysian Heights-Silver Lake, Los Angeles, California, USA, drawing © Chris Reed and Stoss Inc.

Didion, Joan. "Letter from Los Angeles." *The New Yorker* 66, no. 2 (1990): 87.

Venice High School, Venice, California, USA, drawing © Chris Reed and Stoss Inc.

Ulin, David L. *Sidewalking: Coming to Terms with Los Angeles.* Oakland, California: University of California Press, 2015.

Galveston

Galveston, Texas Map: City of Galveston, Galveston, Texas, USA, drawing © Chris Reed and Stoss Inc.

Vision Galveston Public Engagement Process, 2019.

Models of Galveston Seawall, Central Galveston Island, Texas, USA, model © Chris Reed and Stoss Inc.

Illich, Ivan. *H_2O and the Waters of Forgetfulness.* Ideas in Progress. London: Boyars, 1986.

Vision Galveston Public Engagement Process, 2019.

Vision Galveston Public Engagement Process, 2019.

Galveston Seawall, Central Galveston Island, Texas, USA, drawing © Chris Reed and Stoss Inc.

Swift, Graham. *Waterland.* Vintage International. New York: Knopf Doubleday Publishing Group, 2012.

St. Louis

Map: City of St Louis, St. Louis, Missouri, USA, drawing © Chris Reed and Stoss Inc.

Baldwin, James. "Letter from a Region in My Mind." *The New Yorker* 38, no. 45 (1962): 59.

Chouteau (now Brickline) Greenway Framework Plan, St. Louis, Missouri, USA, drawing © Chris Reed and Stoss Inc.

Chouteau Greenway Public Engagement Process, 2019.

Jahren, Hope. *Lab Girl.* New York: Knopf Doubleday Publishing Group, 2016.

Chouteau (now Brickline), Greenway Framework Plan, St. Louis, Missouri, USA, drawing © Chris Reed and Stoss Inc.

Chouteau Greenway Public Engagement Process, 2019.

Green Bay

Map: City of Green Bay, Green Bay, Wisconsin, USA, drawing © Chris Reed and Stoss Inc.

McPhee, John. *The Control of Nature*. 1st ed. New York: Farrar, Straus, Giroux, 1989.

Wooden Origami 1, CityDeck, Green Bay, Wisconsin, USA, model © Chris Reed and Stoss Inc.

Cole, Teju. *Blind Spot*. First ed. New York: Random House, 2017.

Wooden Origami 2, CityDeck, Green Bay, Wisconsin, USA, Drawing © Chris Reed and Stoss Inc.

Ann Arbor

Map: City of Ann Arbor, Ann Arbor, Michigan, USA, drawing © Chris Reed and Stoss Inc.

Mathur, Anuradha, Dilip Da Cunha, and University of Pennsylvania. School of Design. Preface. *Design in the Terrain of Water.* First ed. United States] : [Philadelphia, Pennsylvania]: Applied Research Design Publishing ; University of Pennsylvania School of Design, 2014.

Bench Profiles, Eda U. Gerstacker Grove, University of Michigan, Ann Arbor, Michigan, USA, drawing © Chris Reed and Stoss Inc.

Cole, Teju. *Blind Spot.* First ed. New York: Random House, 2017.

Drainage Plan, Eda U. Gerstacker Grove, University of Michigan, Ann Arbor, Michigan, USA, drawing © Chris Reed and Stoss Inc.

Appearance and (Aesthetic) Experience: The Ongoing Project of Stoss by Julia Czerniak, all photos in this article © Julia Czerniak. Drawings © Chris Reed and Stoss Inc.

Detroit

Map: City of Detroit, Detroit, Michigan, USA, drawing © Chris Reed and Stoss Inc.

Cole, Teju. *Blind Spot.* First ed. New York: Random House, 2017.

Detroit Future City Models, Detroit, Michigan, USA, models © Chris Reed and Stoss Inc.

Jahren, Hope. *Lab Girl.* New York: Knopf Doubleday Publishing Group, 2016.

Detroit Future City, Detroit, Michigan, USA, drawing © Chris Reed and Stoss Inc.

Boston

Map: City of Boston, Boston, Massachusetts, USA, drawing © Chris Reed and Stoss Inc.

Brodsky, Joseph. *Watermark.* 1st ed. New York: Farrar, Straus and Giroux, 1992.

Moakley Park, South Boston, Boston, Massachusetts, USA, drawing © Chris Reed and Stoss Inc.

Moakley Park Vision Plan Public Engagement Process, 2019.

Mostafavi, Mohsen, and Harvard University. Graduate School of Design. *In the Life of Cities.* Zürich: Cambridge, MA: Lars Müller; Harvard University Graduate School of Design, 2012.

Harvard Science Center Plaza Benches, Harvard University, Cambridge, Massachusetts, USA, drawing © Chris Reed and Stoss Inc.

ORO Editions
Publishers of Architecture, Art, and Design
Gordon Goff: Publisher

www.oroeditions.com
info@oroeditions.com

Published by ORO Editions

Author
Chris Reed

Photographer
Mike Belleme

Editor(s)
Chris Reed, Mike Belleme

Editorial Supervision
Patsy Baudoin

Image Supervision
Benjamin Rasmussen

Production Assistant(s)
Alysoun Wright
Sonny Xu
William Baumgardner
Sophie Elias
Koby Moreno

Book Design
IN-FO.CO (Adam Michaels, Shannon Harvey, Marina Kitchen)

Managing Editor
Jake Anderson

Project Coordinator
Alejandro Guzman-Avila

10 9 8 7 6 5 4 3 2 1 First Edition

ISBN: 978-1-951541-44-6

Color Separations and Printing:
ORO Group Ltd.
Printed in China.

ORO Editions makes a continuous effort to minimize the overall carbon footprint of its publications. As part of this goal, ORO Editions, in association with Global ReLeaf, arranges to plant trees to replace those used in the manufacturing of the paper produced for its books. Global ReLeaf is an international campaign run by American Forests, one of the world's oldest nonprofit conservation organizations. Global ReLeaf is American Forests' education and action program that helps individuals, organizations, agencies, and corporations improve the local and global environment by planting and caring for trees.